The Paper and the Pew

How Religion Shapes Media Choice

Myna German

UNIVERSITY PRESS OF AMERICA,® INC.
Lanham · Boulder · New York · Toronto · Plymouth, UK

Copyright © 2007 by
University Press of America,® Inc.
4501 Forbes Boulevard
Suite 200
Lanham, Maryland 20706
UPA Acquisitions Department (301) 459-3366

Estover Road
Plymouth PL6 7PY
United Kingdom

Library of Congress Control Number: 2006938325
ISBN-13: 978-0-7618-3621-6 (paperback : alk. paper)
ISBN-10: 0-7618-3621-7 (paperback : alk. paper)

Contents

List of Tables

Foreword

This book is based on a cross-cultural study of three groups: Mormons, Orthodox Jews and Methodists. The purpose of this research was to determine whether religious minorities, typically mentioned less frequently and believed to have a more insular life, had different experiences as consumers of the newspaper.

As a journalist, the author set out on a journey where she visited many houses of worship in a northern suburban area outside New York City, trying to uncover how congregants related to newspaper purchase. The daily paper was important in the household where she grew up, and despite the Internet and television, was still a regular morning ritual.

She intended to explore differences between the behavior of religious minorities (such as Mormons and Orthodox Jews) and mainstream Protestants (such as Methodists), in terms of newspaper gratifications. As with all journeys, things were not always as they seemed at the outset and the predicted dichotomy did not hold. Instead, she found marvelous distinctions between those actively involved in spiritual life and those who favored a different type of communal involvement.

As a communications researcher, she set out with a series of hypotheses, but the center did not hold. What emerged instead was this book. It is a study of religion within more sheltered communities; it is also a study of media habits within contemporary American society.

It originated with the belief that religious insularity and degree of ingroup identification (presumably stronger) in the minority communities would lead to newspaper aversion and limit its utility primarily to gaining public affairs information, rather than fulfilling some of the "parasocial" functions of media, such as socialization, escape, entertaining oneself.

These are some of the socially accepted uses of media by most individuals. However, devout clusters emerged which were remarkably similar in their newspaper habits and rituals, regardless of their distinct spiritual ties. In affluent suburbia, no group was that insular, in terms of minority outlook and ties affecting media choice. This book is the result of a pilgrimage by one lone journalist seeking information on the spiritual quest and how it affects the conventions of modern life.

Acknowledgements

This book is dedicated to my parents, Leatrice and Hyman German, without whom none of this would be possible.

I thank my colleagues at Delaware State University, Dover, who supported me in this work.

I wish to thank members of my doctoral research committee, Danie du Plessis, Ph.D., and Michael Sabiers, Ph.D., who have been there since the beginning.

Chapter One

Background

"My faith is an important part of my life, as I feel everyone's should be, but I'm always on a spiritual journey. The media is just one source of information, often to be questioned."

—Methodist Congregant, Westchester County, New York

"I care about world events and about people who live outside my sphere. But I learn about it through other reading and discussion beyond the newspaper, which I consider to be shallow, biased and disturbing."

—Mormon Congregant, Westchester County, New York

"Filling in little boxes hardly begins to deal with true feelings. You are treading on sacred ground when you ask us these questions."

—Orthodox Jewish Congregant, Westchester County, New York

1.1 INTRODUCTION

The many racial, ethnic and religious subcultures within the broader American culture have distinctive media consumption patterns (Wright, 1986:137–138; DeFleur & Ball-Rokeach, 1989:188). In a multicultural society, it is important to understand how differences in background and the life of self-contained communities affect how media messages are received (Collins, 1997:109).

The backdrop against which mass communication occurs—the cultural, communal milieu—is believed to have a unique influence on its reception (Stout & Buddenbaum, 1996:20–21; Wright, 1986). DeFleur & Ball-Rokeach (1989:187–190) note that, even before World War II, comparisons of individuals' media consumption behavior revealed that people selected different content from the media and interpreted the same message in different ways.

A scientific study of contemporary media usage patterns could be undertaken based upon social class, gender, age and a multitude of variables, producing many interesting results. These have been discussed in great detail; religion, however, has been underreported. This research focuses on two variables: (1) religious behavior / belief and (2) ingroup identification / cohesion, as factors predicting newspaper consumption.

Past research shows a linkage between involvement in the house of worship and the way media is used (Stout & Buddenbaum, 1996:26). Furthermore, while many studies exist investigating newspaper audiences according to standard demographic variables (e.g., Reina, 1995), few exist that segment the audience by religious preference or degree of religiosity (Stout & Buddenbaum, 1996:5).

Trade groups, such as the Newspaper Council of America, conduct yearly surveys in which they analyze readership along many categorical lines. For example, surveys typically find that newspaper readers tend to be older (over age 50), college graduates and higher-income individuals (Buddenbaum, 1994:17, Reina, 1995:24; Weaver & Buddenbaum, 1980:371–380).

While media surveys have typically asked questions about race (e.g., African-American) and ethnicity (e.g., Italian-American), religion is frequently seen as off-limits to audience researchers. The Superbowl, for example, attracts the largest television audience of any regular program, estimated by Nielsen studies at about 86 million individuals (Hedstrom, 2003). Many demographic facts are known about this audience and it is the topic of many scholarly and commercial media studies. However, questions were never asked as to whether audience members attend Jewish, Catholic or Protestant houses of worship. Religious preference has emerged as the last taboo in audience research (Hoover & Clark, 2002).

1.2 THE EXAMINATION OF RELIGION IN OTHER STUDIES

"Community ties" research studies have found that communities are composed of "joiners" and "isolates" (Merton, 1950; 1983:51–55). The same people participate heavily in a house of worship, join community boards/civic associations, and subscribe to the newspaper (Stamm & Weis, 1986).

The Lynds' (1929:474–475) "Middletown" study of a typical USA community in Indiana described the habit professionals had of arising early, reading the morning newspaper before going to work, relying on information to function better on the job. Factory workers, by comparison, arose earlier, left quickly for work, returned home exhausted and favored the evening newspaper. The newspaper connected individuals to the social life of the town. Berelson (1949:112–188) found that regardless of white- or blue-collar status, anyone deeply involved in local life had to read the newspaper.

Buddenbaum (1993), with an emphasis on religion, repeated many aspects of the Lynds' studies in the same Indiana community, Muncie, camouflaged as "Middletown" in the Lynds' work. She attended church services, compiled information on clergy opinions, interviewed congregation leaders, and surveyed average members at six churches chosen to represent a broad range of Christian theology: fundamentalist, conservative evangelical, mainstream mainline, high church mainline, peace and Catholic.

A Jewish synagogue and a Church of Jesus Christ of Latter-Day Saints (hereafter called "Mormon") existed, but the focus of Buddenbaum's study was Christians. Mormons do not show up in her survey data because there were so few in town that the chance of including enough in her sample to analyze was miniscule. There was also no congregation comparable to the six chosen for in-depth review.

The six congregations were selected primarily from among those included in previous Middletown studies to "represent the conservative-liberal spectrum in Christianity and a particular approach to politics and the world." (Buddenbaum, 1993a:9).

This book aims to explore the life of apparently insular minority religious communities with a high degree of ritualized observance and rules, with a need for self-segregation to ensure conformity to practices, particularly Orthodox Jewish (the most observant branch) and Mormon (apart from Utah, the "headquarters" state), not investigated that thoroughly in past studies. It does not examine the viewpoints of the more numerous but less observant branches of Judaism known as Conservative, Reform and Reconstructionist.

The central hypotheses are that, due to minority status, adherents might choose relative insularity from the broader secular community and the uses and gratifications they get from the newspaper would be different.

Buddenbaum, concurrent with her 1993 study of clergy use of news in "Middletown" pulpit sermons, produced a study of her hometown Colorado newspaper subscription audience, also measuring those audiences for religiosity factors. She found that Merton's (1950) linkage between frequent churchgoers and active community participants ("joiners") could be extended in a three-way relationship with newspaper reading in the contemporary setting. A core group of active residents, she found in Fort Collins, Colorado, were regular worshippers, "joiners" and readers with one exception: Christian fundamentalists, clustered in a few churches, who often attended services several times a week, yet rarely participated in local events and almost never subscribed to the newspaper (Buddenbaum, 1999).

Buddenbaum's (1992, 1993, 1994) research provided the theoretical spark behind this investigation. One could speculate: If Christian fundamentalists withdraw from newspaper use to preserve separate ideas and identity, might not other minority groups, such as Orthodox Jews and Mormons, stressing a religious lifestyle and ingroup identification, also withdraw?

It is important to note that withdrawal may take many forms, but Orthodox Jewish and Mormon texts do not necessarily dictate abstention from newspaper reading. A correlation between various religious groups' response to the newspaper based on theological dogma and adherence to it would need to be undertaken through separate studies with a different design.

This research does not concern itself with theological orientation nor claim to review the numerous studies indicating media use patterns based on church theology. Rather, it is more the social aspect of withdrawal and the insularity of religious communities that is the focal point.

1.3 FOCUS ON ORTHODOX JEWS AND MORMONS AS MINORITIES

Orthodox Jews are a growing segment of the Jewish population. Heilman & Cohen (1989) note the movement of many secular Jews back to orthodoxy, focusing more on traditional observance. Many rules exist within Orthodox Judaism, which serve to enforce a separate identity. For example, rules have evolved regarding mixing of milk and meat and of avoiding ties with secular communities that could dilute religious standards (Rushkoff, 2003:11–13). These rules are not followed as avidly by other branches of Judaism; rather Orthodox Judaism dictates strict adherence. These rules often urge adherents to avoid many venues of secular social interchange, creating a sense of isolation. For that reason, Orthodox Jews were chosen for the study rather than the other three branches' members.

Even though there may be no *de jure* prohibition against interacting with other faiths, *de facto* conditions of daily living promote insularity of both minority faiths.

While possessing an expansionist mindset, an American frontier ideal, nineteenth-century Mormons stressed religious separatism and were persecuted on that account. Non-Mormons, disbelievers in the prophecy of Joseph

Smith and the Book of Mormon, were called "gentiles," viewed as the "other," or "stranger" (Ostling, 1999).

Mormons, like Orthodox Jews, also have strict rules that may result in greater isolation from the mainstream of society. For example, Mormon youth in the New York area must attend a morning religious school from 6 a.m. to 8 a.m. before public school begins. While this may not be a burden in Utah, where the majority of the population is Mormon and a child is not alone in observing this requirement, in the New York area this constitutes radically-different behavior and contributes to a feeling of being an "outsider" (Ostling, 1999). It is the identity the "outsider," rather than the theology, that this research views as creating isolation and a heightened sense of minority (i.e. different) status.

The original hypotheses revolved around finding significant distinctions between the religious majority and the religious minorities, who might be underrepresented in newspaper audiences for the same reasons that fundamentalists are underrepresented. This would hypothetically lead to less community involvement and newspaper use, replicating and extending Buddenbaum's (1999) findings on fundamentalists, adding a second set of exceptions to the nexus of high worship-participation, high community-participation and high newspaper-use.

While developing this research, a plan evolved to use Methodists as surrogates for what journalists call the "man on the street." This reflected the idea that, with clergy endorsement, congregations of Methodists might be more accessible than street-interviewees. Methodists would also constitute a comparable research group, along with Orthodox Jews and Mormons, in that they had chosen house of worship membership and attendance at a particular time.

1.4 CREATING NEW LINKAGES BASED ON PAST LITERATURE

Tables 1 and 2 indicate the linkages that emerged in past research. The goal of this research is to investigate whether, although their degree of fundamentalism is not known, Orthodox Jews and Mormons, as minority groups with the need for self-segregation and withdrawal, conform more to the model illustrated in Table 2. If the hypotheses are supported, Methodists (as a majority group) could be expected to conform to the paradigm in Table 1.

If the hypotheses are supported, the two extreme religious minorities, replete with rules and the need for higher ingroup identification and self-segregation to observe these rules, would resemble the fundamentalist pattern Buddenbaum (1999) observed, as shown in Table 2.

Table 1.   Established Paradigm

Heavy Service-Attendance	→	High Civic Participation Rate	→	High Newspaper Usage Rates

Source: Stout & Buddenbaum (1996:15)

Table 2.   Alternative (Fundamental) Concept Linkage

Heavy Service-Attendance	→	Low Civic Participation Rate	→	Low Newspaper Usage Rates

Source: Buddenbaum (1999)

A similar pattern, akin to the fundamentalist pattern, may be displayed by Mormon and Orthodox Jewish respondents as a result of their minority status and more insular position in the broader society. The "outsider" status connected to being a minority could have a link with less civic participation and newspaper use and thus mirror the pattern Buddenbaum (1999) uncovered in her studies.

1.5 RESEARCH PROBLEM

The study was designed to solve the research problem of how religious minorities view media use, particularly the newspaper. The goal was to ascertain whether religious minority status is a predictor of more or less newspaper purchase. Once the newspaper is obtained, another goal is to ascertain whether the average religious minority group member, with close ties to the house of worship due to the community's insular nature, has different uses and gratifications from a majority group member more assimilated into society.

1.6 GROUPS OF LITERATURE THAT ADDRESS THE PROBLEM

Two areas of literature are reviewed, augmenting the studies on "community ties"—leading works on: 1) "minorities"; and 2) "uses and gratifications" theory.

From the "minorities" literature, Tajfel (1978, 1981) emerged as a leading scholar in the field. His viewpoint on the relationship between the reference groups one belongs to (ingroups) and those to which one does not (outgroups), critical to "social identity" theory, contributed highly to the theoretical basis for this research.

"Uses and gratifications" models developed in communication science flushed out the theoretical foundations, providing another tier in what was emerging as a multi-level structure.

"Secularization" theory, also included, addresses the erosion of belief in the supernatural and faith in otherworldly forces (Stark & Bainbridge, 1985:249). Its addition enhanced understanding of the forces of change in the post- 9–11 world.

1.7 USING PRIOR STUDIES TO ENLIGHTEN THE RESEARCH

The research focuses on selection and absorption of the printed word as it appears in newspapers. While studies of other media, such as television and the Internet, may be referred to occasionally, the aim is only to report the latest theory developments. The main focus of this research is newspaper behavior.

Of the three groups studied, Methodists are presented as less insular, traditionally, than Mormons or Orthodox Jews. The two minorities will be presumed to have no significant difference in insularity.

1.8 RESEARCH SUBPROBLEMS

Each subproblem is represented by a set of hypotheses.

1.8.1 Participation in Political/Civic Affairs by the Majority Group Compared to the Minority

This subproblem looks at the linkage between religion (type) and political participation.

H1a: If individuals belong to the majority, mainstream Protestant group, they will participate more in political/civic affairs.

H1b: If individuals belong to the minority groups, they will participate less in political/civic affairs.

1.8.2 Use of the Newspaper by the Majority Versus the Minority Group

This subproblem looks at the linkage between religion (type) and how the newspaper is used.

H2a: If individuals belong to the majority group, they will use the newspaper more for "public affairs."

H2b: If individuals belong to the minority group, they will use the newspaper less for "public affairs."

1.8.3 Service-Attendance and Political Participation

This subproblem examines the relationship between house of worship attendance in the majority group and political participation, compared to the minority group linkage with political participation.

H3a: If individuals attend services more in the majority group they will
also participate more in the community.

H3b: If individuals attend services more in the minority groups, they will
participate less in the community.

1.8.4 Fundamentalism and Newspaper Subscription

This subproblem looks at the link between fundamentalist ideas and newspaper behavior. It also examines trust of the actual ideas uncovered in the newspaper, whether fundamentalist-leaning individuals have less newspaper trust.
It does not imply that members of the minority groups are more fundamentalist than the majority group, unless that finding emerges independently from
the research.

H4a: If individuals believe more in fundamentalist ideas, they are less
likely to read and subscribe to general newspapers.

H4b: If individuals believe more in fundamentalist ideas, they are less
likely to trust what they read in the newspaper.

1.8.5 Social Cohesion and Trust

This subproblem addresses issues of ingroup identification. It looks for a linkage between high ingroup identification, stronger social ties networks and
less dependence on outside media for news interpretation.

H5a: If individuals belong to a group whose doctrine stresses social cohesion and ingroup ties, they are less likely to read the general press and more
likely to rely on ingroup sources for interpretation of news events.

H5b: If individuals belong to communities with high ingroup ties, they are
more apt to turn to clergy for interpretation of news and current events.

1.9 RESEARCH METHODOLOGY

This research aims to investigate contemporary religious, social, and cultural
communications trends in society through a non-experimental research design.

The primary instrument is a written questionnaire, administered at
churches and synagogues from three faiths. This constitutes a purposive

sample, focusing on attendants at services and evening cultural events (Chapter 4).

1.10 CONSTRUCTS THAT FORM THE BASIS OF THE HYPOTHESES AND KEY CONCEPTS

The terms "concept" and "construct" have similar meanings: a "construct" is a concept, but it has been consciously invented or adopted for a specific scientific purpose (Kerlinger, 1986:27). Scientists loosely call the "constructs" variables and these are the foundations for the study. Each of the variables will be defined as used in the study and operationalized for purposes of statistical analysis.

1.10.1 Religion

Religion is one of two major independent variables emphasized as influencing the behavior under observation: newspaper readership. It has two subcomponents: (a) Type of religion and (b) Degree of religiosity.

In Funk & Wagnall's *New International Dictionary of the English Language* (1987:1064), *religion* is defined as: "A belief binding the spiritual nature of man to a supernatural being, as involving a feeling of dependence and responsibility, together with the feelings and practices which naturally flow from such a belief; any system of faith and worship, the *Christian* religion; an essential part of the practical test of the spiritual life."

1.10.1.1 Type of Religion

Kerlinger (1986:26) characterizes some variables used in behavioral research as true Boolean dichotomies, characterized by the presence or absence of a property (e.g., male/female, alive/dead), while others are polytomies. He cites religious preference as a good example of a polytomy: Protestant, Catholic, Jew.

Religious preference is an independent variable in that subjects enter the study in an "untreated" state. They have either consciously chosen or been born into a particular denomination and entered the study in this manner (in much the same manner as gender), which remains unaltered. They belong and pay membership dues (or each denomination's equivalent) to a particular house of worship, and that categorizes them as a Mormon, Orthodox Jew or Methodist. It is the act of belonging to the denomination and official membership in that house of worship which constitutes religious preference.

1.10.1.2Degree of Religiosity

Within each house of worship, varying degrees of religiosity exist at the attitudinal and behavioral levels. At the attitudinal level, the construct of high religiosity includes strong belief in God as a supernatural being, which is
probed through statements such as a negative reaction to "I doubt the existence of God." A highly religious person would "strongly disagree" with such
a sentiment in a rating scale.

At the behavioral level, the construct of high religiosity is defined by high
frequencies in service-attendance per week, reading Scriptures on one's own
and participating in religious education activities.

1.10.2 Ingroup Identification

An *ingroup* is defined as "any group considered by any of its members to
have a certain exclusiveness: contrasted with outgroup (Funk & Wagnall's,
1987:652). Identification can be defined as (627) "anything by which identity can be established; (psychoanalytic) a process by which an individual,
usually subconsciously behaves or imagines himself behaving as if he
were a person with whom he has formed an emotional tie." In circumstances of high ingroup identification, members maintain their exclusivity
status compared to outgroups and derive their self-image from the tie to the
group, much as they would with another individual in an institution such
as marriage.

At the operational level, ingroup identification is measured by scales of
similar questions probing what actions respondents would take if their group
were threatened and the degree of friendship preference within the group.

1.10.3 Secular Newspaper Consumption

This is the major dependent variable in the study and deserves further
examination.

The word "secular" can be defined as (Funk & Wagnall's, 1987:1138): "Of
or pertaining to this world or the present life; temporal; worldly; contrasted
with religious or spiritual; not under the control of the church; not concerned
with religion, not sacred."

This adjective is used in this study to focus on readership of general circulation newspapers, such as *The New York Times,* rather than publications such
as *The Jewish Week,* also widely circulated in the New York area. While the
study of religious newspapers is certainly important, it is outside the param-
eters of this research.

"Newspaper" can be defined (Funk & Wagnall's, 1987:854) as "a publication issued for general circulation at frequent intervals: a public print that circulates news."

"Consumption" is defined as "the use and consequent destruction of goods in the satisfying of people's needs" (Funk & Wagnall's, 1987:281). At the operational level, it has two subcomponents: (a) reading a newspaper and its associated frequencies, measured in times per week; and (b) purchasing a newspaper, as measured through "subscription" or "non-subscription" on a regular basis. An individual could be high in newspaper reading (several times per week) but not subscribe, preferring to purchase it at the commuter train station or at the workplace. In general, however, subscribers express a more dedicated interest in that they have chosen to pay at stated intervals and have it delivered to the home.

1.11 CHAPTER ORGANIZATION AND KEY POINTS

Chapter Two details "community ties" research that was the basis for this study, along with material on "social identity" theory. "Secularization" theory, a subset which helps shed light on the phenomena of religiosity in a society where it is not always highly valued, is described in the section on "community ties" research.

Chapter Three expounds on the history of "uses and gratifications" research, shedding light on why it is a cornerstone of this study and its relationship with the theories in Chapter Two.

Chapter Four explains the research methodology, the pilot study and how the questionnaire evolved. The actual questionnaire is in Appendix A.

It also explains the factor analysis undertaken to measure the constructs. The statistical techniques by which the factors were formed appear in this chapter.

Chapter Five explains the results of the study, the many findings that the research generated, outside of the hypotheses. While hypotheses may or may not hold, the descriptive findings provide many rich insights and grounds for future research.

Chapter Six presents a conclusion to the research.

Table 3 illustrates the primary concepts used in this research and their connection. The major independent variables are religion (C1) and ingroup identification (C2). Individuals enter the study with a set religion (type) and ingroup identification. The dependent variable (C3) is believed to vary with (C1) and (C2). The aim of this study is to learn more about the variance.

Table 3.   Relationship Between Independent and Dependent Variable Constructs

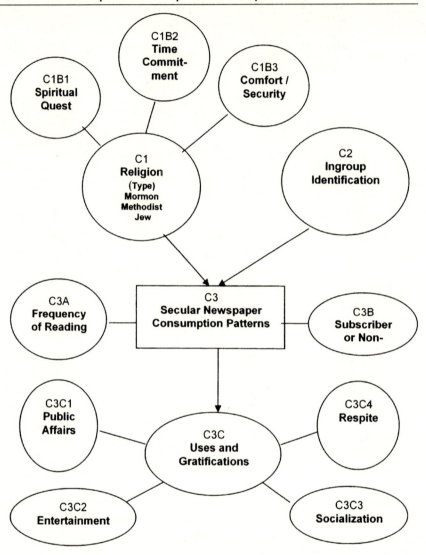

Chapter Two

Social Identity and Community Ties Theories as the Basis for Understanding Minority Group Interaction with the Mainstream

2.1 INTRODUCTION

Two theoretical viewpoints will be introduced as a means of understanding the theoretical base for the study. The focus of this empirical research is how a member of a religious minority may use the newspaper. Issues related to minority group status are explored in this chapter. An explanation of "uses and gratifications" theory is put forth in Chapter 3.

This chapter offers an explanation of various "social identity" theories, positing why they cannot be used to supplant the "community ties" tradition, in terms of understanding minority newspaper readership. The material on "community ties" research also includes information on "secularization" theory.

Each theoretical viewpoint will be explained in terms of its key concepts and its potential to be a bridge toward understanding whether religious minorities will use media differently and have different gratifications.

2.2 SOCIAL IDENTITY THEORY

"Social identity" theory seeks to explain the interplay between the individual and the various membership groups to which he belongs (Tajfel, 1981). These groups can be religious, political, ideological or racial, and the individual can affiliate with varying degrees of intensity: their communality is that they all contribute to a sense of self-definition, place and "identity" in society.

This theory seeks to explain modes of self-classification, cleavage to one's group (whether a majority or minority group) and feelings of superiority or inferiority associated with ingroup membership compared to outgroups (Tajfel,

1978, 1981). At the individual level, it focuses on a person's need to rate highly the groups to which he belongs above the other groups, reducing "cognitive dissonance," reflecting Festinger's (1957) theories (Tajfel, 1981:27).

At the communal level, "social identity" theory examines the relationship between groups, probing into status hierarchies and means of resolving conflict. From there, it can be expanded to broaden one's perspective on general social behavior (Abrams & Hogg, 1990:1–3).

2.2.1 Framework of Social Identity Theory

"Social identity" theory focuses on the interrelationships between various groups, and how individuals view others in different subcultures and segments of society. It offers insights on the juxtaposition of various religious, ethnic and gender minorities in a complex society from a structural viewpoint (Tajfel, 1979, 1981). This is particularly useful in understanding multicultural societies (e.g., South Africa, USA, Australia).

Tajfel (1981:223) notes that very disparate groups with unique viewpoints are "shackled together (in the sense that the fate of each of them depends, to a large extent, upon the nature of its relations with the others)." He develops levels of theory to explain the complexity of these interrelationships.

Many of these disparate groups are religious, self-segregating to maintain unique ideologies in a world they perceive undervalues the religious lifestyle and point of view (Armfield, 2003). Some of these groups are extreme minorities in multicultural societies, compared to European societies of the past, such as France, where most individuals were Catholics.

Since so many societies are multicultural, one could invoke "social identity" theory to explain extreme minorities' media behavior, which could differ from that of majority groups. Since one could posit that members of extreme religious minorities are apt to participate less in the broader society (Buddenbaum: 1992, 1994) and coalesce more at a homogeneous house of worship, one could deduce that they would rate their ingroup higher and maintain some distance from society as a whole, a generalized outgroup, avoiding mass media messages.

Tajfel (1981:xii–7) maintains that it is "large-scale processes" that channel behavior into negative modes such as prejudice, rather than inter-individual conflict or intrapersonal malaise. Thus, "social identity" theory examines the make-up of society and its institutions as a totality, rather than casting blame on unique individuals and their personality structure, for catastrophic world events such as the Holocaust.

Following this line of argument, "social identity" theory would look at how the German body politic has viewed "outsiders" historically as the roots of prejudice, Aryan supremacy movements and the Holocaust, rather than at Hitler's personality or economic events. In Tajfel's terms (1978, 1981), the ingroup would be the Aryan majority and the outgroup the Jewish minority, creating an "us" and "them" mentality that sparked the Holocaust.

He writes (1981:7): "Nearly forty years later, we have seen many new massacres and also some new holocausts." His personal experience as a World War II refugee became the driving force behind his academic interpretation of history (1981:1–6) and his pivotal role in shaping "social identity" theory.

The theory could be summarized as a web of interlocking ideas regarding "self-conception as a group member" (Abrams & Hogg, 1990:2) "Social identity" theory assigns a central role to the process of categorization which partitions the world into comprehensible units and hence contributes to an orderly understanding of self and society.

2.2.2 Ingroup versus Outgroup Derogation

Those studying intergroup relations analyze behaviors that result whenever "individuals belonging to one group interact, collectively or individually, with another group or its members in terms of their group identification" (Sherif & Sherif, 1953:69).

When two groups interact, the group to which a given individual belongs is designated by psychologists as that person's ingroup, while those outside the group are part of the outgroup (Brown, 1998).

"Ingroup favoritism" exists when individuals rate highly their ingroups and maintain neutrality to outgroups. Group members become ethnocentric and overestimate the achievements of their ingroup. This favoritism can be "unconscious" and automatic (Brown, 1998:44–45).

Ingroup favoritism can be broken down into three forms (Brown, 1998:43):

- "Ingroup overevaluation,"
- "Intergroup differentiation" and
- "Outgroup derogation."

The first, "ingroup overevaluation," has been tested empirically by giving subjects in experiments lists of ingroup associated words and outgroup-associated words and asked to rate these words as positive or negative in association. Unconsciously, subjects rated the words connected to their group as positive in connotation (without the association being made conscious) and the words connected to the "outgroup" as negative in feeling (Brown, 1998:44).

"Intergroup differentiation" occurs when individuals rate their ingroups highly and are slightly derogatory to outgroups. When psychologists conducted experiments with high- and low-status participants, however, they found a result that surprised them: subordinate groups exhibit more hostility and bias than higher-level groups. This can be due to their difficulty maintaining a positive self-concept in their situation and a higher need for bonding in the subservient position (Brown, 1998).

"Outgroup derogation" occurs when individuals remain neutral to their ingroup while acting in a highly derogatory way to outgroups. It is not that they have such a positive opinion of their own group; rather they hold to insular feelings (without a positive self-concept connected to their group) and act negatively toward others. This behavior often involves active hostility. It is especially likely when the ingroup is threatened (Branscombe & Wann, 1994:643–645).

2.2.3 Link with Dissonance Theory

"Dissonance" theory is important to "social identity" theory because it strives to relate individual functioning to group functioning. In order to feel better about oneself, it is necessary to elevate the groups to which one belongs, to avoid "cognitive dissonance" (Festinger, 1957).

"Cognitive dissonance" is a theory of "attitude formation and behavior describing a motivational state that exists when an individual's cognitive elements (attitudes, perceived behaviors, etc.) are inconsistent with each other, such as the espousal of the Ten Commandments concurrent with the belief that it is all right to cheat on one's taxes; a test which indicates that persons try to achieve consistency (consonance) and avoid dissonance which, when it arises, may be coped with by changing one's attitudes, rationalizing, selective perception, and other means" (Psybox.com Dictionary, 2003).

Wanting to maintain a positive self-identity, the individual deduces, "If I think highly of myself, and I belong to a group, therefore the group must be highly-rated" (Puddifoot, 1997).

The link between the two theories is that healthy individuals, those with a positive self-concept, will participate in groups of many types and think highly of those groups, in order not to experience discord with their self-concept. The group could be as value-neutral as membership in a health club; if the individual belongs, he rates it highly. It need not have superior moral status or beliefs: avoiding discrepancy is simply a part of positive self-concept.

"Social identity" theory reflects upon Festinger's (1957) "social comparison" theory and unites it with work on self-categorization, comparing particular groups with other identifiable social groups (Puddifoot, 1997:2).

Festinger's notion of social comparison (1957) is that a positive self-concept is critical to psychological integrity. Avoiding isolation, the individual joins social groups, integrating his personal identity with that of the group (Tajfel & Turner, 1986:40). Identity ebbs and flows: at some times, the individual sees himself as *unique*; at other times, he sees himself as a member of a *group*, and both are equally valid to self-construct (Abrams & Hogg, 1990).

However, an interplay exists, since the healthy individual with a positive self-concept tends to rank the groups to which he belongs disproportionately higher to avoid cognitive dissonance (Festinger, 1957). He does not want to see himself as a "loser" and acts to maintain a roseate self-concept. The same individual will assign a lower status to groups other than his own to maintain overarching distinctions and enhance self-worth (Puddifoot, 1997:342–343).

Festinger's dissonance theory (1957) addresses the idea of individuals' filtering information to comport with pre-established attitudes, ideas supported by their group. His theory states that individuals tend to avoid information that is dissonant or opposed to their own point of view and seek out information consonant with, or in support of, their own attitudes.

An interpretation of how individuals read newspapers in close-knit religious communities could draw on Festinger's (1957) dissonance theory. Wanting to maintain a compatibility with group ideology, they could simply screen out the articles that disagree with their groups' viewpoints, so as not to have to reassess their own positions. Using Festinger's theory, it is possible to deduce that ingroup identification and loyalty could lead to non-purchase of newspapers, avoiding discordant truths through non-reading rather than having to screen out divergent information using a perceptual filter on-the-spot.

Behavior comes to reflect an individual's membership in a self-reference group and that group's position in the panoply of other groups that interact regularly in a carefully defined social space (Tajfel, 1981). Each group strives to maintain a distinctive identity and place for itself within the social and political system of a country. Members locate themselves within the norms, boundaries, goals, purposes and social contexts of the groups to which they belong.

2.2.4 Subgroup Status Hierarchy

Fletcher and Fitness (1996) note that individuals bias both attributions and evaluations in ways that favor relationship partners or ingroup members above or close to them. Indeed, a blurring of boundaries seems to occur between the self and ones with whom they most belong. The most significant ingroups and dyads become incorporated into the representation of the self (Brewer & Gardner, 1996:85–87). Individuals assign a status to the groups and dyads to which they belong compared to other units.

An individual belongs to both membership groups and reference groups. A membership group is a group to which a person actually belongs (i.e. Kiwanis, religious organization), but a reference group is that group which is employed as a standard for evaluation of a person's own position (e.g., social class rank). People may use their own membership group as their reference group (e.g., "Methodist Church," "Mormon Church") compared to socioeconomic status (e.g., salary, education level). Research has found that people are satisfied or dissatisfied with their lot in relation to a reference group (Kidder & Stewart, 1975). If the reference group is reading newspapers avidly, it could then be viewed as a desired behavior and acted upon favorably, or the reverse situation could materialize.

Hornsey & Hogg (2002:203) conducted experiments which found that the higher ranked subjects' ingroup, the more apt they were to identify with it, when offered the option of non-identification. While a fundamental human drive is to see the ingroup as positively distinct from other groups, it is not blind, mechanistic or irrational, but affected by reality constraints and status. Since individuals belong to multiple groups whereby they can differentiate themselves, they are likely to cognitively switch their basis of differentiation depending upon the comparative context.

However, Hornsey & Hogg (2002:204) caution that if boundaries are relatively open (as with religion compared to race) those seeking identity enhancement and social mobility might choose to exit their ingroup psychologically and seek membership in a higher-status outgroup. If boundaries are closed, group members have little alternative but to accept low-status group membership.

Vanbeselaere & Boen (2001:765) also discuss the permeability of boundaries and possibility of individuals moving out of low-status into higher-status groups. In keeping with theorists Taylor & McKirnan (1984), they believe that perceived permeability of boundaries leads to preference for individual mobility over collective action. If individuals can escape their group, they have less incentive to work to change social conditions surrounding the group.

Doosje, Spears & Ellemers (2002:57) also emphasize the dynamic nature of group identification, changing over time with environmental situations. Anticipation of a better future for the self and fellow group members is apt to increase the sense of group affiliation, while a view of a dim future might extinguish affiliative ties. Identity-threats increase the salience of the intergroup context and the need to respond to threats at an intergroup level. On the other hand, when loyalties are not fixed and boundaries are permeable the individual has a choice whether to fight with the group or change sides in the battle.

Groups attribute different social status to one another based on their position in society. Membership in high-status groups usually contributes to a positive social identity, whereas a negative social identity is generally associated with membership in low-status groups (Rosenthal & Hrynevich, 1985:725).

A need exists to be accepted by membership and reference groups. Individuals often process information and give out social cues about themselves, so as not to face social rejection or find themselves excluded from their group (Gardner, Pickett, & Brewer, 2000:490).

After reviewing the literature in the field, it seems that while the need to be accepted in a membership group is important, there is no reason to believe that it affects newspaper purchase and use. Members of majority or minority groups could find reasons to use or avoid a newspaper based on other identities, such as needs of their profession.

2.2.5 Roots in the Minimal Groups Paradigm

The genesis of "social identity" theory springs from experiments with the "minimal groups" paradigm, whereby subjects are *randomly* assigned to groups, yet rate their ingroup higher in all categories than relevant outgroups to maintain a favorable self-concept (Vanbeselaere, 2000:516–518). Categorical memberships, albeit arbitrary in the experiments, get internalized, become integrated into participants' self-concepts, causing them to rate themselves and their group higher than other groups, while no objective difference exists.

The "minimal groups" paradigm's tenets have been substantiated in studies with both adults and children (Puddifoot, 1997). When there is no apparent distinction between groups and subjects have been situated in groups with no apparent rationale, they still state that their group is superior. When this concept is applied to religious or ethnic minority groups, the majority or plurality group thereby can always find some reason why it is better or superior to the minority and act upon it politically (Tajfel, 1981).

Diehl (1990) & Turner (1981) conducted experiments whereby groups were formed on relatively trivial criteria to test the efficacy of the Minimal Groups paradigm in specific settings. Upon assignment to a group, people appear to think automatically of that group as better for them than any alternative outgroup. This is due to their desire to keep a positive self-image. Puddifoot (1997:343) maintains that there is a tendency to distort perceptions of the outgroup, in line with self-image management.

Hartstone & Augoustinos (1995) believe that the "minimal groups" paradigm results in ingroup bias when two groups are involved, yet not when three minimal groups are involved. The prejudice and distinctions that result from a two-group design diminish when more groups are involved. Moving along this dimension, it could be maintained that prejudice is higher in a society obviously split along two categorical lines than in a multi-ethnic or multi-racial society in which polarization of the two groups is less likely.

Applying the "minimal groups" paradigm to the New York City area, the site of this empirical study, one could speculate that there is less intergroup hostility because the society is inherently multi-racial, multi-ethnic, almost more so than in any other place in the nation.

A situation does not exist where only one or two groups predominate, as expressed by Harstone & Augoustinos (1995). There would therefore be less propensity to rate other groups lower than one's own, since there are so many ratings that would have to be assigned to develop a pecking-order for one's own and other groups. This could be contrasted with a bipolar society such as Québec in Canada, where the English and French have maintained a lifelong hostility, or Northern Ireland with the Protestant/Catholic feud.

Brewer (1979) investigated the "minimal groups" paradigm through experiments whereby participants were categorized randomly and anonymously, without having face-contact with other groups or prior experience with their categorizations. In these experiments, participants always rated their groups higher, whether in intelligence or other positive attributes, even though they knew nothing about the people in the other groups, their backgrounds or abilities.

Brewer concluded (1979:318–320) that mere categorization elicits behavior that favors ingroup members relative to outgroup members. Tajfel & Turner (1978, 1986) incorporated this thinking into their theories on social categorization, viewing groups as striving for positive ingroup distinctiveness and identity based on their own needs rather than rational competencies.

The "minimal groups" paradigm became the conceptual springboard against which Tajfel (1978) developed his theories on group behavior. He created a new gestalt in psychology that shifted worldwide attention away from pre-existent individualistic explanations for prejudicial behavior toward social-causality modes.

Growing out of the "minimal groups" paradigm tradition and moving toward a broader-based "social identity" theory, Tajfel (1978, 1981) posited that participants identify with minimal groups and compare them with relevant outgroups to protect or enhance self-esteem. He then made a case for focusing attention on the group as the unit of analysis, while previous scholars had looked to *individual* prejudice as the root cause of negative attitudes towards other ethnic and religious groups.

Tajfel & Turner (1986) popularized the notion that ingroup favoritism at the cognitive level results from an individual's need to have a positive self-concept. This prompts the person to seek and maintain some kind of distinctiveness from the outgroup by promoting the ingroup to which he belongs.

"Social identity" theory, linked integrally with Tajfel's work, maintains that social identity is clarified through social comparison, but generally it is between ingroups and outgroups. Accentuation of differences occurs between ingroups (e.g., "ours" is smarter or more hard-working) compared to the outgroup which is disparaged (Abrams & Hogg, 1990:3)

Tajfel (1981:255) defines social identity as referring to "that part of the individual's self-concept which derives from their knowledge of membership in a social group or groups, together with the value and emotional significance of that membership." Individuals will characteristically categorize people in such a way as to favor members of the group to which they themselves feel they belong compared to other group, maintaining positive self-identity at all costs.

Berger (1966:106–107) wrote: "Society not only defines but creates psychological reality. The individual realizes himself in society — that is, he recognizes his identity in socially defined terms and these definitions become reality as he lives in society." In other words, people will view themselves as defined by others. If others view their religious or racial group negatively, they are apt to adopt the oppressors' view of themselves, unless events happen at the individual level to boost their self-concept (e.g., they are appointed to a court or Cabinet position, despite their circumstances of birth).

"Social identity" theory examines groups and the structure of society (Tajfel, 1981). Functionalist theories such as "uses and gratifications" (Dominick, 1990) of media also focus on how an individual expresses himself through media choice: it is possible to correlate both theories and determine if a more religious individual has a specific media choice; it is possible to determine if a more ingroup-identified individual has a specific media choice. It is not possible to determine whether their decision to be religious or irreligious, ingroup-identified or not identified, reflects societal prejudice toward their denomination or group.

2.2.6 Ethnocentrism

Ethnocentrism is the "point of view that makes the social group to which a person belongs the center of all things in that person's world, and elevates the group above all other possible groups. The group in question may be race, nationality, sports team or indeed any other form of social grouping" (Psybox.com Dictionary, 2003).

Ethnocentrism has historically led to group members' overemphasizing the achievements of their ingroup (Basu, 1999:1), even before the advent of the "minimal groups" paradigm and "social identity" theory. As a group focuses on the larger differences between itself and an outgroup, it heightens mutual attraction and solidarity within the ingroup (Kidder & Stewart, 1975).

Sociologist George Simmel (1955:17) notes: "a certain amount of . . . outer controversy is organically tied up with the very elements that ultimately hold the group together." In other words, external turbulence and even discrimination foster identity within the group that then needs each other to survive and creates social bonds.

Many ethnic groups in various societies are persecuted minorities and need one another to survive. Many complex societies consist of nothing but minorities, whether professional, regional or political. Tajfel (1981:187–191) notes that they maintain belief systems and self-conscious identifications that make them unique. The important political and existential question becomes whether or not the ethnocentrism is necessary for survival of the group or whether it becomes the basis for unnecessary one-upsmanship with other groups.

Ethnocentrism is more common in minorities (Brown, 1998:75). Simpson & Yinger (1985:17) note:

Minorities are subordinate segments of complex state societies; (2) Minorities have special physical or cultural traits which are held in low esteem by the dominant segments of the society; (3) Minorities are self-conscious units bound together by the special traits which their members share and by the special disabilities which these bring; (4) Membership in a minority is transmitted by a rule of descent which is capable of affiliating succeeding generations even in the absence of readily apparent special cultural or physical traits; (5) Minority peoples, by choice or necessity, tend to marry with the group.

Minority groups within any society struggle to maintain group identity and cohesion in the face of dangers. They control their members through a shared system of beliefs which are inculcated from members' inception into the group (Galanter, 1989: 98–99).

A group's needs are met by the overall behavior of the membership and adhesion to common goals (Von Bertalanffy, 1952). Group cohesion is the result of all forces acting on members to keep them engaged in the group (Galanter, 1989:99). The loss of distinctive identity, historically, is feared more within minority communities than within the majority group.

The potential loss of identity through intermingling and adopting certain media choices could be studied through ingroup-identification scales. What is not discernible is whether media are avoided by insular religious minorities to avert absorption of broader societal norms. There could be many reasons why media may be avoided, but "social identity" theory does not offer any clues as to these causes. Since this study was not a content analysis of media, asking respondents to analyze media text for topics which challenge group norms, it could not address challenges to group assumptions once the newspaper is in-hand. Rather, it addresses more frequency and regularity of buying a newspaper than specific reaction to viewpoints expressed in that newspaper.

Billig (2002:173) takes issue with the "blood-and-guts" model of conflict allied with ethnocentrism, a sense that all groups are threatened by the existence of "outsiders," noting that even Tajfel (1981) believed that there are rational reasons for social psychological biases. Both scholars believe that while all individuals can display hostility toward groups other than their own as a function of cognitive processing, this does not have to lead to outright warfare.

In prejudiced, ethnocentric thinking, Billig (2002:174) argues, judgments are made about members of outgroups regardless of individual characteristics. Members of the outgroup are judged negatively or unfavorably stereotyped simply because they belonged to the outgroup. Tajfel (1978) related this type of stereotyping to ordinary sense-making of the world, the need to create cognitive shortcuts to categorize the plethora of information that assails the individual everyday. As to whether ethnocentrism has to create bigotry, its most extreme form, both scholars walk an equivocal line, suggesting a confluence with historical conditions to create genocide and holocaust situations.

2.2.7 Self-Categorization

Social identity is "self-conception as a group member" in a community (Abrams & Hogg, 1990:2). It is a means of self-categorization. A psychological sense of community, tied to place and position in society, has come to characterize healthy individuals in all cultures. Within the context of the larger society, individuals self-categorize to locate themselves within smaller groups (Wright, 1986).

Suzuki (1998:158) believes that belonging to a group is largely a psychological state, distinct from that of being a separate individual, giving the person social identity. A configuration of theories evolves from accepting this understanding, but at its core is the emotional need of the individual to experience himself as part of a larger whole. In order to maintain this loyalty, ingroup members may distance themselves from outgroup members in their communication patterns.

Clinical psychologists use the term "identity" to refer to understanding oneself as an individual, with personal goals and values (Baltus, 1988:89).

The "personal identity" construct refers to self-descriptions, in terms of intellectual and physical and personality traits. One could view oneself as "talented, artistic or gifted"—these are personal traits.

The "social identity" construct relies on self-descriptions in terms of social category memberships, such as race, religion, class, nationality and gender (Bornman & Mynhardt, 1991). Using this construct, an individual may view himself through the lens of race ("I am black," "I am white") or religion ("I am Jewish," "I am Mormon"). The salience of these traits, how important each is to the particular individual, may vary given the society he lives in and the relative importance that society places on race or religion at a given time. An identity that may seem relatively unimportant at one time in history may become crucial at another point.

Concerns about self-identity can be found simultaneously on several levels, each varying in salience at a particular point (Capozza & Brown, 2000:33). Individuals belong simultaneously to several groups: religious, professional, avocational. The strength of their identification with each will shape their actions. Or, given the situation, a particular affiliation could become dominant.

2.2.8 Stereotyping and Prejudice

Tajfel (1981)) believes that the categorization process leads to harmful stereotyping and prejudice on the part of the majority group. He views the categorization process as a cornerstone of aggression by ingroups against outgroups and the basis for close ingroup networks.

Tajfel explains very comprehensively (1978, 1981) how social ties (group membership) influence the individual and collectively determine the social setting of a society. However, he cautions that the overall social climate and degree of perceived conflict in the world, rather the danger level, will influence an individual's adhesion to his group.

In more turbulent times in the broader society, the individual will cleave more to his own group. Yet it is precisely that cleavage and the closed-in quality of these groups that provokes aggression and jealousy in the broader society, particularly if one closed-in group enjoys unprecedented affluence or other privileges (Tajfel, 1978).

"Social identity" theory maintains that group identity threats should increase intergroup discrimination, with the greatest external threat instigating the highest level of discrimination (Worchel & Coutant, 1998). Threats to the ingroup in the environment should excite concerns with intergroup comparisons, thereby affecting ingroup identification and influencing responses to both ingroup and outgroup.

2.2.9 Stereotyping

Stereotyping often occurs when groups are threatened. The "other" or out-group is accorded negative stereotypes, which are often compounded through mass media (Kreps, 1990:50–51). This often impinges on the ability of members of the outgroup to develop a healthy self-concept.

By understanding ingroup identification and outgroup dynamics, in conjunction with mass media, professionals can learn to adopt better reporting mechanisms and stem the tide of prejudice.

2.2.10 Depersonalization and Dehumanization

Turner (1999) appears to dismiss prejudice and stereotyping, viewing "depersonalization" of the other as the crux of poor intergroup relations. He writes (p14) that depersonalization is the basic process that "produces group behavior" and that "psychological group formation is an adaptive process."

The individual uses stereotypes to put the people he encounters daily into consistent categories, and that, in itself, is not repugnant in a society with massive information processing demands (Turner, 1999:15). It is more the mechanistic, impersonal way that the "other" is looked at, in his mind, that is problematic. This shifts the emphasis from Tajfel's concern that prejudice and stereotyping are social problems at the individual, perceptual level. Billig (2001:80) notes that dehumanization even occurs in ethnic jokes, where the "other" is depicted as less than human.

2.2.11 Religion as a Social Identity

Religion has been selected as a form of social identity in part due to its variability in expression under crisis or non-crisis conditions and the belief in inherent spirituality coloring the human experience. The degree of religiosity (not the type), particularly in the case of those seeking "comfort," one of Buddenbaum's (1994) classifications, could rise and fall with changes in the world situation.

Being religious is an identity, but it is an identity that is able to shift, unlike race or gender. It is based more on inner attributes rather than fixed demographic classifications. For example, as a Protestant, one can join a particular denomination and go regularly during one life-stage or historical period; one can join another denomination or have a different service-attendance pattern under other conditions. Hence, religiosity, with its shifting identities, has been less studied in its relationship to media compared to other, primarily demographic, sources of identity.

2.2.12 Why Social Identity Theory needs Augmentation to Explain Religious Identification

The decision to be an Orthodox Jew, the branch of Judaism with the most rules and requirements, constitutes an act of faith and commitment (Heilman & Cohen, 1989). Therefore "social identity" theory could not be invoked solely to say that a person chooses a religion (type) or avoids it due to others' perceptions or rankings of the group or degree of prejudice. Orthodox Judaism existed even under the most prosecutorial conditions, such as the Holocaust, when one would think abandonment would occur. One could not say that a believer was guided to become part of this particular ingroup by attributions of higher- or lower-status.

Being a Mormon often correlates with regionalism in American society: most Mormon Church members descend from the original settlers who ventured into the Western states with Brigham Young in the 1840s, originally from British, Irish or Scandinavian backgrounds. While not a minority in western states such as Utah or Idaho, they are definitely a minority in the New York City metropolitan area. They often affiliate with their church to maintain cultural ties with persons from their home states and lifestyle from another part of the country. Again, one could not presume that the desire for higher socioeconomic status by joining a more highly-ranked group would contribute to joining the church, but rather the need to affiliate with others like oneself.

Methodists were chosen for this study as surrogates for the mainstream majority Protestant population. They represent the average American who does not have the constraints of being in an enclosed, self-contained religious community. The purpose in their selection was to have a statistical baseline against which to compare the behavior of minority group members. Their role in the status hierarchy was never in question or under discussion; they were chosen to represent the identity of the typical American without rigid religious constraints or membership in an insular community.

"Social identity" theory concerns itself mainly with how the individual situates himself within the rubric of community, the degree to which he identifies with the group and how his group ranks against the other groups. Once the individual is not highly affiliated with his group in terms of identity, it does not offer an explanation of his behavior.

Religiosity (intensity of devotion) as a component of one's social identity is not examined extensively in the "social identity" literature, which tends to link identity more to culture and national origin. But the "community ties" tradition, as extended and modified examines the reasons for religiosity and opens the door to ranking individuals according to degree of religious impulse.

2.3 COMMUNITY TIES THEORIES

2.3.1 Introduction and Overview

The "Community ties" tradition is pertinent to the study of how insular religious subcultures view the newspaper, since these subunits are part of the patchwork that comprise the broader community. While the original "community ties" theorists examined the broader community, later research made it possible to gain new perspectives on the interaction of smaller sub-communities within the larger framework.

The Lynds (1929) examine "Middletown" as a typical USA community, at a time when most of the population in the smaller cities (i.e., Muncie) was white Protestant. Merton (1950) discusses the role of "joiner" in these cities and notes that some individuals participate more fully in society, volunteering for service on town boards or library committees, and attend church more regularly, while others assume detached roles and become "isolates."

Another group of sociological theorists (e.g., Herberg, Gans, Kanter) published extensive research between 1951–1975, at a time when religion and ethnicity became more common *foci* of analysis. It is this second group of theorists who look at sub-communities more critically, creating the groundwork for Buddenbaum's research (1992, 1993, 1994).

Buddenbaum (1993, 1994) builds on the results of both groups of research with important modification. She begins with acceptance that there is a core of residents in each broader community that plays a pivotal role and forming the basis of leadership groups. To this extent, there has always been a core group more integrated in the community. Granovetter (1978) refers to this group as having stronger "community ties."

Weekly attendance at a house of worship, which allows for even more regular interaction than a sporadically-scheduled town board or library committee meeting, has typically been part of the routine of a "closely-tied," integrated community member. Hence, it could be viewed that there is generally a nexus of overlapping activities for the "closely-tied" community member (Table 1): church attendance, civic participation, newspaper reading.

The newspaper is a communications vehicle uniting a community. Missing the paper, as occurred during a well-research *New York Times* newspaper strike, created a fissure in the social fabric of the community. Attendance at movie theaters decreased, since entertainment offerings and feature times could not be made public through the newspaper. Hence, researchers accept that newspaper use unites a community, informing residents about civic issues and events, and supports greater participation (Berelson, 1949:112–114).

However, since the original "community ties" literature does not address the insularity of subunits of society (sub-communities), it cannot report nuances in the link between church attendance in the broader community, civic participation and newspaper reading, based on religion (type) and the insularity of some sub-communities (Table 2).

2.3.1.1 Extension of the Community Ties Tradition

The second group of researchers (emphasizing sub-communities) created the groundwork for Buddenbaum's studies, since they focused on religion and ethnicity as variables for observation. The earlier theorists focused more on social class as a predictor of group behavior.

In the forefront is Herberg (1955:227), who discusses the "triple melting pot" whereby society engages in a tripartite division according to Protestant, Catholic, Jew. Religion in the average USA suburb emerges as the primary context of self-identification (p47).

Herberg writes (p49):

> Sociologically . . . the religious community has emerged under compelling circumstances to serve as a context of self-identification and social location in contemporary American life. . . When he [an American] asks [about a new family in town] 'What *are* they?' he means to what religious community they belong and the answer is in such terms as 'They're Catholic (or Protestant, or Jewish).'

Herberg (1955) examined each of these sub-communities, in terms of their similarities and differences. In USA suburbs, Herberg deduced that societies were forming along the lines of Protestant, Catholic and Jew.

Each religious group was living parallel-but-similar lives in the post-World War II suburbs, populated by returning soldiers often living apart from their parents in the inner cities. Religion (type) assumed a role as a social force in municipalities. Interfaith groups and committees ensured a certain degree of cooperation and ecumenism. The important dimension was that one belonged and affiliated with a religious group to have a satisfactory "place" in the societal structure.

He writes (p227):

> These three communities stand on the same level, recognized as equi-legitimate sub-divisions of the American people. In another sense, however, they are markedly different—in their historical background, their social and cultural structure, their place in the totality of American life.

Within the social structure of the suburbs, ethnic origins were becoming less important, compared to religion (type). While previously, Irish roots might have been important, Irish-Americans were beginning to view themselves more as Catholics (Herberg, 1955). They would intermarry more with Italian-Americans, also Catholics, but not with Jews.

Gans in a study of Italian-Americans in Boston notes (1962:104) that "sociologists generally use the term 'community' in a combined social and spatial sense, referring to an aggregate of people who occupy a common and bounded territory within which they establish and participate in common institutions."

The specific institutions constituting community are the church, parochial schools, social, civic and political institutions (including some which are church-related). Using ethnographic and participant-observer methods, Gans examines the "peer group" society of the Italian-American and discusses the view toward outside" agencies (those in the municipality, but not the immediate religious-ethnic community).

Sociologist Kanter (1972) created a theoretical breakthrough by studying communities from the perspective of "commitment." Kanter compared contemporary communities (including communes) with their counterparts in the nineteenth century. She writes (p134):

Commitment mechanisms are exaggerated versions of processes that may emerge in all groups . . . including hierarchy, ritual, protection of 'shared truth' from outsiders, extragroup conflict, formal initiation, seclusion, de-individualization.

She continues, in discussing social religious communities (p136):

There are many social practices often associated with religion that were useful in building commitment. These practices include a comprehensive value system and a transcendent moral order . . . religious groups often require shared beliefs and conversion to those beliefs, which may include belief in inspiration, revelation, or nonscientific sources of wisdom.

The social customs of belonging to a group create adhesion and Kanter cites the strong communal ties of alternative communities such as Black Muslims or Hasidic (a form of Orthodox) Jews (p137).

It is the nature of these social ties that create alternate societies within the broader framework, rather than the theology, and the insularity that is proposed to affect media use.

2.3.1.2 Changes in the "Community Ties" Paradigm

A change had occurred in the paradigm of studying communities. The new outlook in the "community ties" mold understood society as a series of cooperating subunits, organized primarily around religion (type).

The original "community ties" literature (Lynd, 1929; Merton, 1950) did not address the subject of various or even competing denominations. It merely examined how society existed as a totality at a given period in time (the 1920s, 1930s, 1940s). It examined the habits of members of different social classes in a community (i.e., the Lynds, 1929), reporting how upper-to-middle-class residents read the newspaper before work, while factory workers went to their jobs earlier and read it (if at all) at day's end. They did not address religion (type) or ethnicity in their study of community, partially because the USA and smaller cities (i.e., Muncie) were less diverse at the time.

Buddenbaum (1993, 1994) approaches the subject matter in consort with later sociologists (e.g., Gans, 1962; Kanter, 1972), examining the habits and viewpoints of individual religious communities. In this sense, it meshes more with the modified viewpoint of "community ties" theorists.

Since the original theorists did not examine religion (type), favoring a social-class orientation to societal understanding, it could be stated that Buddenbaum's work reflects more the updated "community ties" outlook. It is important to note, also that Herberg (1955) did not discuss theological orientation of each religion, or only tangentially, but focused on behavioral aspects, daily living habits of each group, and integration into USA norms.

Stout and Buddenbaum (1996, 2001) are remarkable in the breadth of their research in that they address both social segmentation (i.e., the habits of a Mormon community) and theological dogma differences in creating sub-communities with distinct differences in their view of media. They address television-viewing habits and other media habits, as well as the newspaper.

This book focuses on the newspaper. It relies heavily on Stout and Buddenbaum's work, but it does not seek to determine differences visible through religious-text study and a critical view of theology. This book's central hypotheses focus on the assumption that divergent uses of the newspaper originate from minority-group membership and concomitant insularity.

The fact that Orthodox Jews comprise only 10% of the Jewish community, which is itself only 2–3% of the USA population, seems a fair indicator of minority status. Mormons also share "outsider" status the farther one moves away from their headquarters in Utah in the USA West, approximately 2000 miles from New York City, where this study took place.

In 1993, a Buddenbaum study of a Colorado town (Section 1.2) replicated the results of earlier studies confirming the linkage of high church involvement, high newspaper ties, high civic participation. However, it was innovative in producing a notable exception to the established paradigm (Table 2): A large group of respondents in the study showed outstanding church attendance and involvement, without concomitant high civic participation and newspaper usage rates. Upon further investigation, Buddenbaum found these respondents to the newspaper study shared involvement in conservative, fundamentalist houses of worship. While mainline Protestant results reflect earlier findings, the fundamentalist groups did not show the same correspondence to previously established norms.

Buddenbaum (2001:86) has cautioned:

> With at least 100 churches that are traditionally classified as 'mainline' or 'old line,' it is difficult to say with any certainty what these moderate to liberal Protestants believe about the media or, for that matter, almost anything else. There are differences among mainline churches, denominations, and congregations and differences within them.

With so many congregations and differences (type of dogma) between the Mainline Protestant groups, a theological study of texts could not be conducted for the current study. Methodists were simply chosen as a centrist, bellweather church (Stern, 2001:A1) to represent the world of the mainstream Protestant.

A more isolated approach to community participation was found (Buddenbaum, 1999), to exist within the world of the Christian fundamentalist, proving exception to previously-established norms (Table 2). It was this orientation —the view of insularity needed to reinforce rule-obedience and conformity to norms—in two other minority religions—that the current research study attempts to probe. In that sense, it is a look at the habits of more insular religious communities in secular society.

In including ingroup attachment measures, the current research aims to separate those adherents more allied with their group from those who participate but share less intensity of attachment to their group. That line of analysis depends upon strong confirmation of ingroup attachment differences intra-group (between members) and inter-group (between the three communities).

"Community ties" theory, as it evolved and expanded, still was thought to shed great light on the research problem. It was chosen as a theoretical base in its modified form, since the goal of this research was to address the viewpoint of minority religious communities, subunits of the broader community.

2.3.2 How Community Ties Research Evolution Links with Changes in Research Viewpoints on Media

2.3.2.1 The Chicago School

Since 1910, theorists had been studying communities in the United States, with the Lynds' (1929) Middletown study emerging as the most influential. A group coalesced around scholars at the University of Chicago who viewed the broader community as the fundamental unit of analysis in studying behavior, including media habits. With an emphasis on social class, this viewpoint predominated through World Wars I and II, but was challenged in the late 1940s and early 1950s.

2.3.2.2 The Columbia School

With the work of Lazarsfeld, Berelson & Gaudet (1944) and Merton (1950) in the forefront, a stream of research emerged from Columbia University in the late 1940s and early 1950s that was more social-psychological in nature, using the individual as the unit of analysis.

It was the individual's need for the media that was paramount, and the individual nervous system decided what "uses and gratifications" it set out to obtain. The "effects" paradigm put forth that media had different effects on an individual, based on his needs.

If the need for "stimulation" were salient, the individual would attend to entertainment aspects of a newspaper. If the need to feel attached to society were salient, the individual would attend to aspects of the newspaper that made him feel that he belonged and was not an outsider. At social occasions, the individual could cite this material and show that he was integrated member of the American whole, rather than the sub-community of the block or neighborhood.

This viewpoint shifted the focus from mass media as a broad entity having the same affect on all listeners and viewers to a cohesive channel that affected each person differently.

The individual was viewed as an amalgam of many needs and identities, any of which could become salient at a given time, based on central nervous system processing and the demands of the situation.

2.3.2.3 Post-World-War-II School

By the 1950s, it was also accepted in academic circles that the individual and his central processing system or brain determined how he viewed media. Within that affective system were strong needs for belonging, acceptance and approval (Maslow, 1954).

Concurrent with post-World-War-II USA society development was a massive movement of returning soldiers and their brides from the central cities to outlying suburbs. Since many soldiers settled farther away from their immigrant parents still in the central city and extended family ties were diluted, religious institutions became very important as a social base in broader communities, with affiliations along the lines of Protestant, Catholic or Jew

(Herberg, 1955). This does not imply a "splintering" in pursuing and attending to civic matters.

What developed was a series of tightly knit communities within the main municipal community, sharing common secular newspapers augmented by smaller religious newspapers which served a more specialized religious base.

2.3.2.4 Counterculture Developments

The period 1945–1960 was a time of great growth for all groups, but by the 1960s indifference set in with the "counterculture" (Yinger, 1987). A movement to privatize religion took place, with many people belonging to the "invisible church" (Jorstad, 1986).

In the 1970s, interest among young people peaked in Asian religions and membership in mainline congregations declined. About 4% of the country was involved in the Transcendental Meditation movement (Jorstad, 1986).

The Protestant mainstream had found a way to accept the Catholic John F. Kennedy as president, and became a very important force, together with liberal Catholics and prophetic Jews, in providing religious legitimization to the Civil Rights movement as well as to the anti-war movement of the 1960s and early 1970s. Whether or not they would eventually throw in their vote with Ronald Reagan, mainstream Protestants continued to look with distrust on the Fundamentalists who, they felt, were a threat to freedom of conscience and separation of church and state (Bulman, 1991:530).

Up until the 1960s, the primarily private character of religion dovetailed with the rapid secularization of the country, a phenomenon which, almost imperceptibly, had come to dominate the first half of the century. But as Protestant, Catholic and Jewish clergy locked arms with the charismatic Baptist minister, Martin Luther King, Jr., in protest against the oppression of the black minority, American religion broke the bonds of the restricted, private quarters to which the predominantly secularized culture had previously confined it (Carter, 1993). In the 1970s and post-Vietnam War society, much liberalization occurred, along with intermarriage among ethnic and religious groups.

2.3.3 Buddenbaum and the Types of Religiosity

Buddenbaum (1994) views those actively committed to life in the religious world as having three primary motivations:

- Spiritual quest,
- Comfort/Security, and
- Leisure-time socialization.

Each of the three categorizations in her typology will be discussed. It is important to note, however, in understanding later empirical chapters that statistical findings in this study reflect "factors" as they coalesce in the survey instrument, which mirror but not exactly overlap with Buddenbaum's categories.

2.3.3.1 Religion as Spiritual Quest

Buddenbaum (1994:3) defines a "questor" as "having a religiously inspired world view and desire for belief-confirming information regardless of religious beliefs. In other words, the "questor" is interested in the religious experience *per se* and may even try to be impartial to the "brand" of religiosity, selecting what suits his needs without a firm or exclusive orientation. To that extent, the "questor" is religiously tolerant of other groups.

"Questors" are pro-religious and encompass all denominations. They tend to focus more on spiritual needs and derive satisfaction more related to inner psychological needs than social networking. This group is less likely to participate in temporal affairs and more in spiritual matters, using the house of worship as a base for this orientation.

The most religious of the "questors" often view themselves as "fundamentalist," according to Buddenbaum (1994), avoiding the newspaper and civic activities in favor of an isolated stance that they believed necessary to preserve spirituality in a world driven by secularism.

2.3.3.2 Religion as Comfort/Security

The "religion as comfort" orientation taps an intrinsic or God-centered approach to religion (Buddenbaum, 1994). It is similar to the "questor" mentality in that it is inner-oriented rather than societally oriented. Both groups possess characteristics which differentiate them from the more social mentality which in the past has driven an understanding of church attendance and community participation.

The difference between the questor-oriented and the comfort-oriented religious individual is that the questor is open to investigating many different religions and is more of a seeker. The "religion as comfort" mentality revolves around satisfaction within one's faith, viewing it as the religious home, and this person is more of a "finder" than a "seeker."

Buddenbaum (1994:3) views the questor as interested in "mature religion." This individual harbors a desire to view information which both supports and contradicts his religious beliefs. An individual interested in religion as comfort, on the other hand, might rely on religious publications more than secular versions, since they are more apt to support his general outlook.

2.3.3.3 Religion as Leisure-Time Socialization

A congregant who attends the house of worship for social reasons is apt to be involved politically in the community, vote regularly and support public institutions such as the newspaper or library. Buddenbaum (1993:2) notes that individuals who attend to news are more active in the political process. This argument is well-taken, in that if one is well informed through the newspaper, one is most apt to participate in the community (Berelson, 1949; Lynd, 1929).

In the past, going to church or synagogue, constituted a major time-commitment and was often tied to the need to see friends and neighbors. It was akin to being involved in a social club or community activity (Armfield, 2003:13). This group's motivation is more external and need not reflect the need for questing or comfort/security, although there could be some overlap.

When the term "socialization" is used in this research, it does not reflect the degree to which an individual is "socialized" to church teachings; rather it is that person's *use* for religion. Religious affiliation can be used for questing or comfort purposes; it can be used to address social needs and create a link with neighboring citizens.

2.4 LINK BETWEEN COMMUNITY AND RELIGIOUS INVOLVEMENT

Past research (Janowitz, 1952; Merton, 1950) found links between individuals who are more religious and attend church and integration in local communities.

Studies cast in the "communities ties" tradition often rely on worship service attendance as a surrogate measure of community integration. If an individual is a regular churchgoer, he is more apt to be a member of other activities and boards in the community and have a greater need to know about community events (Buddenbaum, 1994:23).

This tradition infers that the integrated individual attends church to be part of the community, greet neighbors and be viewed as a good citizen. It maintains that the same drives that lead a person to join local a public school parents' association motivate the person to attend a house of worship and that a deep desire to belong to the community prompts service-attendance.

However, religion can also be a way of retreating from the world, as observed by Lenski (1963). The use for religion as a restorative wellspring within the individual could determine whether it correlates with these other measures. Lenski found that those whose primary relations *are within* the church community may lean toward *withdrawal*, while those with more significant relationships in the *broader* community are more apt to lean in the directionality of *overlapping* church/civic participation.

Buddenbaum (1994), in a study of multiple allegiances, found a significant statistical variation: a group of respondents said they went to church regularly, even once a day, yet did not participate in political institutions, serve on town boards or subscribe to newspapers. Her results showed that they all belonged to the same church, a group of Christian fundamentalists, seeking insularity. The link between church attendance, community participation and newspaper consumption did not hold with this group.

Conservative Protestantism in the USA tends to foster a more dualistic worldview that encourages withdrawal from the world and its temptations (Hart, 1992:43–81). Church leaders often associate mass media with "the world," which they alternatively condemn (as in the case of television violence) or embrace (when media teach religious values), according to Stout, Scott & Martin (1985).

2.5 OTHER IMPORTANT LINKAGES

2.5.1 Religion and Withdrawal

Stout (2001:7) notes that "religious criticism of popular culture is an essential part of life in many faith communities."

He writes (p9):

> Direct admonitions (against) media are not likely to be found in Reform and Conservative Judaism, which are different types of knowledge cultures . . .

Orthodox Judaism, with its stricter view of insularity, is conveniently excluded from this statement, because it involves its own set of group pressures, strict observance to ingroup norms.

Kosmin (2002:47) notes that Orthodox Jews are more like fundamentalist Christians in many ways, which is why they can be combined with Mormons comfortably in an analytical study.

2.5.2 Fundamentalist Link

Although fundamentalism as a phenomenon does not directly apply to all religious minorities, it is an assumption of this study that some of the traits of fundamentalism may present itself in minority groups included in this study. Minority religions with an insular orientation may mimic the fundamentalist paradigm (Buddenbaum, 1992) and since the mirroring could reflect parallel ideology, this became part of the research and testing process.

Dollar (1973:5) defines fundamentalism as "the literal exposition of all the affirmations and attitudes of the Bible and the militant exposure of all non-Biblical affirmations and attitudes." Central to this view is imagining oneself in the midst of a religious conflict, in which the universe divides into forces of light and darkness.

Orthodox Jews are stricter than the other three branches of Judaism in their observance of rules and more literal interpretation of Scriptures. While the other branches could be seen as less literal, it is suspected that the Orthodox Jewish branch, with its more literal adherence to the Bible (Kosmin, 2002:48), behaves in many of the same ways as fundamentalist Christians. To that extent it could be studied with Mormon and Pentacostal faiths. Orthodox Jews' stricter (more literal) adherence to Scripture creates the possibility of linking them with Mormons (Kosmin, 2002:45). Hence, it seemed appropriate to have Mormons and Orthodox Jews under observation in the same study, while the combination with the other branches of Judaism would not have suggested itself.

2.5.3 Nexus between Fundamentalism and Newspaper Subscription

Some research indicates that both worship attendance and membership in civic groups positively correlates with newspaper subscription (Finnegan & Viswanath, 1988:565). The same individual who goes to church regularly is also likely to participate in other aspects of civic life, has a greater need to know about the community and is more likely than others to subscribe to and use local media to learn about it (Stamm & Weis, 1985; Merton, 1950). Yet, as Buddenbaum's (1994:125) findings show, respondents who held fundamentalist beliefs were significantly less likely to read a newspaper and more likely to distrust its contents.

Two groups of people are crystallizing: those who go to church regularly, but shun civic participation and newspaper reading (often attending for spiritual or withdrawal reasons, including fundamentalists); and those who attend for social reasons, adhering more to the traditional linkage with community participation and newspaper reading.

The need to know about community events will prod the individual to either subscribe or purchase the daily newspaper, Berelson (1949:114) maintains. Missing the newspaper makes an *integrated* community member feel disparate and detached from societal groups, even becoming a source of anxiety (Berelson, 1949:112). However, this begs the question of whether, in spiritually oriented groups, the ideal is seen as being a good member of broader society or devoted spiritualist maintaining ingroup norms.

2.5.4 Minority Group Membership Linked to Non-Involvement

If an individual belongs to a narrowly defined minority group and this is his primary focus or self-categorization, even if a regular churchgoer he may be less involved in the broader community and less apt to purchase a newspaper. In addition, once the newspaper is brought into the home, the use of that newspaper may be different from that of the person more involved in broader society.

Since it might be argued that the minority group member has alternative media that displace the newspaper, which might be equally engrossing and important to him, uses of other media are relevant and may bear light on this discussion.

2.6 INTRODUCTION TO SECULARIZATION THEORY

The basic tenets of "secularization" theory will be explored with a view toward understanding how religious minorities perceive themselves and react to media differently from majority group members. This investigation makes the assumption that the denominational majority will be more secular, because of overlapping roles and loyalties with other civic organizations, compared to minority groups, believed to be more insular.

Secularization theory seeks to understand the retreat mechanisms of minority groups wishing to maintain a separatist ideology in a world that they perceive undervalues the religious lifestyle and point of view (Armfield, 2003:4).

To understand this viewpoint, it is helpful to conceive of society as a polarization between: a) secular values, as represented by mass media, commercialism, the world of work, upward mobility; and b) religiosity, seen as devotion to the house of worship, spiritual goals, a God and the faith community.

Recent findings show mass media use by religious individuals can be explained by "secularization" theory (Buddenbaum, 1986; Stout & Buddenbaum, 1996). These scholars found that religion correlates with newspaper use to varying degrees, with those most active in their house of worship most apt to read the newspaper and participate in community events (Buddenbaum, 1986). However, individuals whose religiosity was primarily motivated by spiritual rather than social reasons lagged behind in their readership and civic participation.

The current secularism in USA society represents an entirely new phenomenon, argues Armstrong (1993: xviii) in *A History of God.* Since the dawn of history, *homo sapiens* has also been *homo religious*. "Men and women started to worship gods as soon as they became recognizably human," she notes.

Early societies such as those of Mesopotamia, Egypt and Greece were organized around sacred duties, the temples and the worship of the gods. Even after the advent of monotheism, religion served as the focal point of the community, with impoverished towns allocating great sums of money to build cathedrals. This outlook lasted in the western world until the end of the nineteenth century (Armstrong, 1993).

With greater industrialization, urbanization and societies united by a media presence ranging from television's development in the late 1940s to the Internet in the 1990s, the sense of the "spiritual" or "holy" which pervades the lives of people in more traditional societies has been essentially eliminated, according to this viewpoint (Armstrong, 1993:4).

Secularization theory states that a strong religious lifestyle has been under attack from secularist society, resulting in a negative correlation between religion and mass media (Armfield, 2003:4). The argument meshes well with "uses and gratifications" theory, which incorporates Festinger's "dissonance" theory (1957), stating that individuals turn to media to reinforce pre-existent values, while shunning media outlets that challenge their values.

The group that fundamentalists view as most challenging their values are "modernists." This group, according to DeLubicz (1978:30), sees the "sacred" as nonsensical, with anti-religious tendencies developing, since science is believed capable of anything. A discontinuity has come to exist between the world of religion and the "sacred," as expressed in close-knit faith communities, and the world of rationalism and modernity, as expressed by the media.

In order to preserve their boundaries and hold the line against "modernists," faith communities such as the Mormons do ask that adherents to eschew media (Stout, 1985). However, the message may not be explicit; it may be implicit. In devoting one night a week to "family home evening," with prohibitions against television, the Mormon Church is implying that media values are anti-family and should be avoided generically. It does not have to spell out that one should refrain from excessive television use during the remainder of the week, as it is implicit in its denotation of that evening as religiously advantageous.

The view of avoiding media to avert subversion and modernity has historical antecedents. The first of many denouncements of mass media by religious institutions began with the Protestant and Catholic Churches during the nineteenth century. They proclaimed that novels should be considered the equivalent of alcohol and tobacco, diminishing religious values (Douglas, 1988).

The Mormon Church is very adamant in its proscription of alcohol and tobacco. In recent years, leaders of the Mormon Church have been increasingly
concerned about the effects of mass media on religious values (Stout, Scott &
Martin, 1996:243). A Mormon respondent to a survey quoted by Stout, Scott
& Martin (1996:249) said: "Anyone who watches it [TV] regularly is not con-
tributing adequately to their home, community or personal lives. . . . The best
two years of our lives as a family were the two years that we did not have a
TV in our home." The implication, although not made explicit, was that a
higher level of spirituality can develop in a home if media use is limited.

The overall rationale driving the study of secularism is, "In the face of scientific rationality, religion's influence on all aspects of USA life—from personal habits to social institutions—is in dramatic decline" (Swatos & Cristiano, 2000:6). Traditional religious beliefs are being replaced by standards
that are more secular, and a new modern lifestyle reflects these values.

Swatos & Cristiano (2000:14) further state: "Pluralism clearly creates a
market-place of ideas where absolute claims for ultimacy are always at some
degree of risk." An atmosphere of pluralism in the USA allows individuals to
freely exchange ideas and beliefs about their faith with people of other faiths,
and in consequence they are more knowledgeable and less defensive of their
own. The pluralistic atmosphere and agreement to allow a marketplace of
ideas diminishes ingroup identification and paves the way for a loosening of
the bonds postulated by "social identity" theory.

Stout & Buddenbaum (1996:20) note: "Secularization theorists expect the
relationship to be negative (for religious people) because mass media is considered part of modern, secular society." But, they argue, this applies only to
people whose motivation is individual-level religiosity. The traditional nexus
of high church attendance with high newspaper reading and high civic participation will remain intact if socialization is the primary motive.

In that sense, this interpretation of secularist theory is "functionalist" in
much the same manner as "uses and gratifications" theory is. Uses and gratifications theory is being invoked by this researcher to look at the functions of
the newspaper. Both theories are compatible in examining the individual as
the unit of analysis; both are compatible in their functionalist outlook.

2.7 SUMMARY

While "social identity" was reviewed in great detail and given much consideration, the reason "communities ties" theory was later invoked as the ultimate prism through which to view the research problem of minority and majority group religious participation and media use is that it supports a possible

differentiation between religious questors (spiritualists without any denominational boundaries) and secular society. The emergence of such a large and influential group of individuals whose particular denominational bias is incidental signifies broader societal trends and a challenge to established ways of thinking.

The "community ties" tradition sheds more light on religiosity and media than "social identity" theory. The latter theory concerns itself primarily with how an individual situates himself within a community, the degree to which he identifies with the group and how his group ranks against the other groups. Once the individual is not highly affiliated with his group in terms of ingroup identification, it does not offer an explanation of his behavior. Furthermore, it does not adequately address religiosity as an identity.

Religiosity as a social identity (being religious or non-religious) is not discussed in the "social identity" literature, which tends to examine identity according to which denomination an individual has joined. The "community ties" tradition, followed by "secularization" theory, had to be invoked to examine the motivation for religiosity and open the door for categorizing individuals by type of religious impulse.

By Buddenbaum's (1994) division of religious individuals into questors and those seeking social satisfaction, categories are created which can be cross-correlated to explain newspaper use. Hence, understanding this tradition has been most useful in developing the ultimate research design.

"Community ties" outlooks reflect a shared spiritual orientation rather than a particular church membership. If fifty questors (those with a spiritual orientation) are placed in a room together, one imagines that they have more in common with each other than with co-religionists who do not share this outlook.

This is apt to influence their media use, creating more remarkable similarities than differences. Thus, it became impossible to use "social identity" theory, with its reliance on ingroups and outgroups as the leading theoretical force in understanding minority-majority group religious behavior. Religiosity could be better explored through "community ties" and "secularization" theories.

"Social identity" and "community ties" theories were both influential in formulating the empirical study. "Uses and gratifications" work (Chapter 3) also provides a base. The research methodology reflects all three sets of theories.

Chapter Three

Needs Analysis of Media Usage Patterns of Religious Communities: The Uses and Gratifications Theory

3.1 INTRODUCTION

The "uses and gratifications" paradigm is a complex web of interwoven social psychological and media theories. Rather than address the media as a unified channel with a distinct message grasped by all consumers in similar fashion, focus shifts to the individual.

If "community ties" theory is the lens through which the researcher examines individual behavior (Chapter 2), "uses and gratifications" theory can be thought of as the roadmap beneath the lens. If "community ties" theory helps us figure out why an individual may go to one medium over another (i.e., *The New York Times, The Wall Street Journal*) "uses and gratifications" theory helps us understand what she does when she gets there and why she does it.

This book examines minority individuals situated in insular religious communities and compares them to mainstream Protestants who, by virtue of their numbers, are more integrated into the USA social system. "Uses and gratifications" theory, compared to other social psychological theories, focuses on the individual as the unit of analysis and then examines the group to which she belongs.

A focus of this investigation is to compare the "uses and gratifications" of media, as categorized by scholars (e.g., Berelson, 1949), experienced by religious individuals with more secular, assimilated individuals. Mass media, it is speculated, could have more affect on individuals who do not derive primary gratifications from daily observance, face-contact and frequent house of worship meetings. In this sense, secular individuals could be considered more alone psychologically and more tied to mass media for gratification.

This chapter discusses the evolution of "uses and gratifications" theory, how it applies to news consumption, and how it applies to insular religious communities.

3.2 REASONS FOR INVOKING USES AND GRATIFICATIONS THEORY

A "functionalist" theory, such as "uses and gratifications," enables the researcher to categorize and study the needs that media fulfill in human life (Dominick, 1990). "Uses and gratifications" theory is "functionalist," according to Blumler & Katz (1974), since it posits that when individuals reach desired media destinations they can engage in any or all of several activities or functions: entertain themselves, gather information, take respite from the hustle-bustle of life (as on holiday) or socialize (with "friends"). These are the uses to which one puts media and the gratifications that one experiences as a result (Korgaonkar, 1999; Rubin, 1984).

In this study, the null hypotheses would of course be that for a strongly religious person the "uses" to which she puts a newspaper and the gratifications she finds there would not be different from those sought by totally secular individuals. But there is some indication in prior studies that this may not be the case (Buddenbaum, 1994; Stout, 1985).

3.2.1 Communications Activities and Media Functions

The earliest uses and gratifications studies (e.g., Lasswell, 1948) posit three major functions of mass media: (1) surveillance of the environment (reporting of news); (2) correlation of the parts of society in responding to the environment (interpretation of information and prescribing conduct in reaction to events); and (3) transmission of the social heritage from one generation to the next and to newcomers, communicating knowledge, values and norms.

Another mass media function is the bestowal of prestige upon individuals who make the effort to stay abreast of news. Often individuals who elect to pay attention to events in society emerge as opinion leaders and appear more as cosmopolitan influentials (Wright, 1986).

From the individual's viewpoint, he has a use for the news itself, but also for the status that comes with being knowledgeable about world events. If a person is knowledgeable about news, he is considered more cosmopolitan; if he is mentioned in the news, he achieves even greater status (Lynd, 1929).

Because human beings are concerned with their image, they tend to solicit opinions from friends and neighbors on important issues, making their own opinion mesh in a way that enhances their status within the group (Wright, 1986).

One's ego, self-image and even psychological equilibrium are bound up in the communicative interaction with other people (Leathers, 1986). Hence, the integrative and interpersonal aspects of mass communications are becoming increasingly important.

Informal networks give a person feedback, whether he is a successful, integrated member of society or marginal to the culture. In addition, these networks serve as grapevines, channels of news, in which media messages get interpreted. In closed societies, these networks assume more importance and their interpretation of news can even supersede the value of the news itself in shaping critical opinions (Kreps, 1990).

3.2.2 Explanation of Audience in Terms of Uses and Gratifications

McQuail (1987:1) notes: "'audience' is a term that is understood by media practitioners and theorists . . . it has entered into everyday usage, recognized by media users as an unambiguous description of themselves." Still, the notion of an audience is completely unsettled and subject to many connotations.

In addition to "functionalist" theory, commentators in the critical studies arena often comment on media messages. While "functionalist" theory is the focus, the critical studies perspective is mentioned although not utilized.

Webster (1998:190–195) explains the three views of an audience: audience as mass, audience as outcome, and audience as agent. In the audience as mass viewpoint, individuals are conceived as scattered across time and space, acting autonomously with little or no knowledge of one another. Individuals are perceived as statistics, and, as Bogart (1996) has observed, this notion fails to study adequately the processes through which audiences ingest material afforded them. The emphasis is on size of the audience and its marketing or demographic characteristics.

The audience as mass model implies passivity, susceptibility to influence (Williams, 1989) and institutional interests. The audience as outcome model, by comparison, reflects concerns about the power of media to produce detrimental effects on individuals (Webster, 1998). The defining question of this outcome model is "What do media do to people?" It concerns itself with propaganda, corporate and political consequences of communication, and is, incidentally, the oldest of the three models.

The notion of audience as agent has attracted interest since the 1970s. Rather than viewing individuals as acted upon by media, they are conceived as free agents, choosing what they consume, bringing their own interpretative skills to the texts they encounter, deciphering their own meanings and generally using media to suit themselves. The preeminent question of this agency point of view is "What do people do with media? (Webster, 1998).

It could be argued that this third outlook, reflecting the notion of the active agent, is rapidly achieving preeminent status in the communication discipline (Webster, 1998).

Perse and Dunn (1998:435–456) put forth a pithy explanation of the contemporary audience as agent viewpoint: media users are actively involved in selecting media content to satisfy certain needs. Because media users are actively aware of their communication needs, they select communication channels/media that they believe will gratify these needs.

3.3 HISTORICAL DEVELOPMENT OF USES AND GRATIFICATIONS THEORY

3.3.1 The 1940s and 1950s

"Uses and gratifications" theory originated in the 1940s in social psychology and was adopted into communications through the work of Bernard Berelson (1949). During a newspaper strike in New York City, he investigated "what missing the newspaper means" to various people. He found, for instance, that the newspaper provided a social venue for most people, apart from transmitting world views. Individuals felt less connected to the community without the newspaper. They attended fewer cultural events, including movies, because they were not aware of their existence or starting times.

Berelson (1949:112–114) categorized the reasons people read a newspaper as:

- Information,
- Socialization,
- Public Affairs
- Entertainment and
- Respite.

These became the benchmark classifications and the basis of all future "uses and gratifications" research.

In the 1950s, social psychologist and humanist Abraham Maslow popularized the needs hierarchy (1968:168–170) which accesses individuals developmental functioning, as they seek survival, security, belonging and self-actualization goals. As individuals progress up the ladder, as lower-level needs are met, they begin to seek experiences that fulfill higher needs. Having secured food, they start to seek intellectual and cultural experiences that fulfill longings for status, belonging and self-actualization.

Applying Maslow's theory, media users, depending on their level of psychological development, mood-state or status in the community, have different goals. An individual situated at the highest developmental level, seeking self-actualization, may read the newspaper to be an educated, intellectually enlightened person. Someone functioning at the level of "survival" may read it only to find evidence of sales, ways to save money or find cost-cutting coupons. The newspaper, the medium, is unchanged. It is the consumer's "use" for it, this researcher maintains, which is different.

The views of Maslow, while put forth in psychology, have been adopted into many disciplines, reinterpreted and reapplied. Maslow himself does not specifically apply his theories to the communication discipline or "uses and gratifications" outlooks.

In the 1940s and 1950s, mass media were seen as all-powerful, determining how audiences think. Individuals were seen more as robots, to be manipulated, coaxed and coddled.

3.3.2 The 1960s and 1970s

By contrast, the viewpoint of a passive audience faded with the revolutions of the 1960s and 1970s. With social change, an idea sprung forth that the audience actively selects media that fulfill its needs.

Mass media consumption was not something done to people, forced upon them against their will, in the new viewpoint, but something they actively sought. The active-recipient assumption reversed the notion of great, influential media plying their wares on mindless victims. Essentially, it was the audience that became empowered. Much of the history of the 1960s, ranging from the Civil Rights Movement to the Vietnam protests, was about citizen empowerment, and media studies reflect this viewpoint, this researcher maintains.

Blumler & Katz (1974) discuss the use of media in terms of the gratification of social or psychological needs of the individual. The mass media, they contend, compete with other sources of gratification, but offer exceptional value from their content, due to familiar daily formats and repeated exposures. This is in line with the counterculture's emphasis on individual fulfillment in that era.

The "uses and gratifications" perspective is utilized frequently to examine audience uses of mass media according to social and psychological needs. It implores scholars to think of media exposure as an intervening variable in the study of traditional communication effects research (Katz, Blumler & Gurevitch, 1974).

The "uses and gratifications" approach contends that the audience goes to the media for specific gratifications, using the mass media rather than being used by the mass media (Cassata & Asante, 1979). It attempts to bridge the gap between media functions and user needs.

3.3.3 The 1980s and 1990s

This era differs from past epochs in communications research in that mood and individual personality structure are thought to account for media effects. Zillmann (1983) points out the overwhelming influence of mood on media choice: boredom encourages investment in exciting content; stress encourages the choice of a relaxing context. Purchasing the same newspaper, for instance, may gratify different needs for different individuals. Different needs are associated with individual personalities, stages of maturation, backgrounds and social roles.

Palmgreen, Wenner & Rosengren (1985) view audiences as differing in the gratifications they seek from the mass media, but these orientations are related to social conditions, personality dispositions and abilities. These orientations result in assorted media use patterns and a variety of media effects.

Denis McQuail (1987) puts forth the following typology of common reasons for media use:

• Information, finding out relevant events and conditions in immediate surroundings, society and world; seeking advice on practical matters;
• Satisfying curiosity, learning, self-education, gaining security through knowledge;
• Personal identity, finding reinforcement for personal values, finding models of behavior;
• Integration and social interaction, gaining insight into the circumstances of others, empathy, a sense of belonging, finding a basis for conversation and social interaction, connecting with significant others;
• Entertainment, relaxing, escaping, being diverted from problems, filling time, and emotional release.

McQuail draws on the audience as agent model, actively seeking out information, participating in his fate, not being manipulated by the power of the media nor passively alone, unlinked to fellow man in a sea of media appreciation.

Williams (1989) simplifies McQuail's typology into five motivations for using media:

• The need for human contact, not feeling alone, relating to others;
• Surveillance needs, information;

- Social or cultural needs, belonging;
- Escape, release from problem thoughts;
- Personal identity, learning more about self, outright pleasure, positive arousal.

3.3.4 The Humanistic Challenge to Uses and Gratifications Theory in the 1990s

While "uses and gratifications" theory has been comfortably situated in the social sciences, a new stream of research has arisen in the humanities tradition that seeks to understand the same phenomena. Reimer (1998:134) notes that qualitative methodologies such as reception analysis and ethnography are developing important insights on the viewpoint of an audience.

This approach, sometimes referred to as "reception theory" or "reception analysis," focuses on what people see in the media, on the meanings which people produce when they interpret media "texts" (e.g., Ang, 1985; Seiter *et. al.*, 1989).

This perspective tends to be associated with the use of interviews rather than questionnaires. Such interviews are often with small groups (e.g. with friends who watch the same TV shows). The emphasis is on specific content (e.g., a particular news show) and on specific social contexts (e.g., a particular group of working-class women viewers).

The qualitative approach studies the meaning, semiotics, attached to media viewing rather than developing quantitative characteristics of an audience, such as Nielsen statistics based on black boxes installed in televisions measuring viewing-hours. While this is a challenge to "uses and gratifications" theory, it is very much outside the realm of this investigation. The use and frequency of newspaper readers' efforts is under study, not the meaning they attach to the newspaper.

3.3.5 Twenty-First Century Research

In the most recent "uses and gratifications" research, Sherry (2001) attempts to link inborn genetic traits with media choice. Recent advances in psychobiology provide a new way to address the question of etiology.

Sherry (2001:276–277) notes that most research to date has ignored the issue of etiology and has focused on creating motivation typologies. His research showed that temperament, inborn personality, was a consistent and moderately strong causal factor underlying television use. Particularly potent predictors of television use motivations were negative mood, low-task orientation and behavioral rigidity.

Sherry is not referring to negative mood causing a person to engage in prolonged, television use on a given day; rather, he refers to lifelong brain factors as a predictor of extended-hours sitcom use versus human interaction. Similarly, he maintains that individuals with low task-orientation, not moving toward concrete goals, are more apt to spend repetitive, idle hours in front of the television set, rather than working on projects. Behavioral rigidity, a precursor of obsessive-compulsive disorder, predicts extended television use based on habit and avoiding the need to make flexible choices in terms of expenditure of personal time.

A key characteristic of twenty-first century research is that it looks at the mentally balanced individual not just in humanistic psychology terms but in terms of biochemical balance terms.

3.4 USES AND GRATIFICATIONS THEORY: BASIC ASSUMPTIONS

"Uses and gratifications" theory assumes that different individuals have different uses for the media. It assumes that communication is a social process, fundamental to human survival. Through the process, individuals develop and maintain a working consensus about the social order. Without repetitively engaging in acts of communication with fellow man, no one could develop the mental processes and social nature that distinguish humans from lower forms of life (De Fleur, 1970).

"Uses and gratifications" theory expands upon the basic tenets of communications theory, that messages spring from media sources and are interpreted selectively by audiences with unique psychological needs.

Mass communications evokes images of radio, television, the Internet, but these are technical devices, only instruments facilitating what is fundamentally a human process (Wright, 1986). Individuals tap into media systems for a variety of reasons.

Research data has led to assumptions about the human personality, and a scholarly literature has developed in social psychology and anthropology, which has filtered into communications theory. "Uses and gratifications" theory embodies assumptions from all three disciplines, while applying them to the media.

Williams (1989) draws on these assumptions to situate "uses and gratifications" theory under the broader aegis of the effects paradigm. "Uses and gratifications" theory negates the view that the human being is helpless, a victim of a media barrage. Williams assumes that the audience member, rather than being passive, is actively involved in searching out messages that support his current needs. Messages extraneous to those needs will be ignored.

"Uses and gratifications" theory assumes that individuals seek pleasure over pain and will seek media that foster positive emotions. Consumers seek the stimulation of exciting new ideas, feeling high positive arousal, achieving a "peak" experience or a feeling of transcendence through media or literary venues. Examples include a stirring novel, story, film or television show.

This theory makes the assumption that, given the distinctly different needs of individuals at a given time, they will seek out different media. Even within the context of the same media (i.e., reading a newspaper), their orientation will be determined by their place in a given social group. Some communities will favor receiving news from an outside source directly, while others favor the filtering process of the community and opinion leaders.

3.5 APPLICATION OF USES AND GRATIFICATIONS THEORY TO NEWS CONSUMPTION

One area that has been explored using historical methods and the "uses and gratifications" approach is news media consumption. News has important implications in the creation of an informed electorate in areas including politics and international events (Vincent & Basil, 1998).

According to the "uses and gratifications" approach, predispositions such as an interest in current events drive news media use across the various media (Wenner, 1986). This approach also states that gratifications obtained will drive media use. Gratifications achieved, combined with actual hours of media use, determine current events knowledge (Vincent & Basil, 1998).

Cumulative research suggests that audiences seek and receive multidimensional psychological gratifications from each media content type (e.g. Internet news viewing can satisfy surveillance and respite needs, among others). These audience behaviors point to a relatively utility- or goal-oriented viewing public (e.g. Levy & Windahl, 1985).

A Katz, Gurevitch & Haas study (1973) found that newspapers best serve the needs of integrating people into the socio-political order; books best serve the need of knowing oneself; and television offers the escape motive. It could be presumed that reading news on the Internet has the same function as newspapers.

3.6 THE USES AND GRATIFICATIONS THEORY AND THE INTERNET

While newspaper reading is the focus, much recent research extending "uses and gratifications" theory has selected the Internet as its application vehicle.

Many of the theoretical concepts apply to newspaper reading and hence are presented, although the Internet is not the focus of the empirical study.

The consensus among scholars is that the "uses and gratifications" approach is well suited for studying computer-mediated communication such as Internet use (e.g., Eighmey & McCord, 1998; Newhagan and Rafaeli, 1996; Rafaeli, 1986).

Surveillance needs, for instance, determined adoption of news and information activity from videotext systems, a precursor to today's online services (Lin, 1993).

Lin (1993:224) summarises the basic assumptions of "uses and gratifications" theory as follows:

> The Uses and Gratifications perspective . . . assumes that media use behaviors are motivated by certain internal needs and specific gratification-seeking motives. With such self-fashioned intentions, audiences are able to dictate their content selection and use patterns for the purposes of fulfilling their gratification expectations.

The "uses and gratifications" theory also provides a theoretical explanation for changes in media usage-patterns following the adoption of new communication media. Perse and Dunn (1998:437) maintain that this theory also helps to explain the displacement of functional alternatives. That is, existing or outdated media channels can be replaced by new alternatives to fulfil similar needs. Hence, the Internet has replaced many of the socialization and information functions of the newspaper.

Lin (1999) discusses how the rising power of the Internet and online services is eroding the television audience. The Internet is also eroding newspapers' power over textual news material. Large numbers of people who formerly read newspapers are getting much of their current news material on the Internet.

A recent industry study indicates that online audience-activity is motivated by the same factors: the need for gratifications in escape, entertainment, interaction and surveillance (Miller, 1996). The technology is different, but the needs are the same.

Korgaonkar (1999) identifies seven factors that motivate Web use:

- Social escapism, similar to entertainment, allowing the individual to relax, overcome daily boredom and stress or overcome loneliness (much as with television);
- Privacy in financial transactions;
- Information motivation (using the Web for self-education and information needs);

- Interactive control motivation (personalizing and customizing experience to fit exact needs);
- Socialization (facilitating interpersonal communication and activities, sharing knowledge with friends about information and socializing through e-mail, bulletin boards or chat rooms);
- Non-solicited privacy motivations; and
- Economic motivations for collecting information, such as trading in stocks, bonds or other investments.

3.7 MEDIA SUBSTITUTION EFFECTS

According to the media-substitution theory, audience members may substitute the use of a functionally similar medium for another when such a substitution need arises and the circumstance presents itself. The classic example of this type of media-substitution dynamic is the displacement of radio by television as the most widely adopted mass entertainment medium (Lasswell, 1948).

Althaus & Tewksbury (2000) found that use of the Web as a news source is positively related with reading newspapers but has no relationship with viewing television news. Consumers will substitute using the Web for purchasing a newspaper to read news, but once a decision is made to use broadcast versus text-oriented channels, a different sensatory mode has been selected and substitution effects do not apply.

A different playing field exists for a more active, reading news mode, or passive viewing mode. Web use hinges on familiarity and comfort with computers, according to Althaus & Tewksbury (2000). They expect the choice between the Web and traditional media to hinge on a person's level of comfort with computer technology, and thus anticipate that computer anxiety could mediate the choice between new and traditional news outlets.

Online news sources appeal to those with relatively high levels of political expertise or sophistication, a finding confirmed by 1996 American National Election Studies data (Davis & Owen, 1998). A similar pattern was observed in a study examining the choice between traditional newspapers and video-text services (Heikkinen & Reese, 1986:20–24).

The Heikkinen & Reese study found that people with a low need for information based their choice on familiarity with the two media, with older people more likely to choose newspapers and younger people the electronic medium. People with a high need for information, on the other hand, tended to adopt both.

3.8 LINKS BETWEEN USES AND GRATIFICATIONS, SOCIAL NETWORKS AND CLOSED COMMUNITIES

While "uses and gratifications" theory focuses on the individual, it addresses social networks through Berelson's (1949) view of the newspaper as a socialization tool whereby individuals connect to others through media. Missing the newspaper means that an individual temporarily feels disconnected from society.

Members of closed communities perhaps feel less "disconnected" in day-to-day life, since religious observance creates much face-contact at services and meetings. Thus, they are apt to be more satisfied with the interpersonal nature of their lives than non-religious individuals and may need the media less for connectivity purposes. They might, for example, need the Internet less as a connective tissue, since they belong to a face-community with great contact.

Turkle (1996) indirectly supports this viewpoint, with information on how Internet users seek to "reinvent themselves," trying out relationships in online communities. People in closed communities, more socially connected, perhaps have less reason to "reinvent themselves"; and, if they do so, the tendency is to move away from the community physically.

Kraut & Attewell (1997) identify information-seeking and the need for instaneous rewards as the two significant predictors of overall satisfaction with the Internet. Since the Internet has massive databases, with links and references to any topic imaginable, it makes sense that information-seekers would find it fulfilling.

3.9 CRITICAL EVALUATION OF USES AND GRATIFICATIONS THEORY

Criticisms of "uses and gratifications" theory run the gamut, ranging from the quantitative work in the audience studies mode being too cerebral or administrative in orientation, to charges of logical positivism from critical studies believers. Qualitative audience studies, are often criticized from the statistics-oriented researchers as too ungeneralizable, since individuals ascribe different meanings to the media they consume (Webster, 1998). Both types of researchers, audience studies statisticians and critical studies scholars searching for meaning in messages find fault with each others' methodologies.

The use of retrospective self-reports, which is common in "uses and gratifications" research, has several limitations. Media users may not know why they chose to employ the media they did or explain it rationally. The reasons that they articulate, may, in fact, be the least important. People may simply offer reasons that they have heard other individuals mention.

Some degree of selectivity of both media and content is clearly exercised by audiences (e.g. choice of Internet content). However, instrumental (goal-directed) accounts assume a rational choice of appropriate media for predetermined purposes. Such accounts over-emphasize informational purposes and ignore a great deal in people's engagement with media: newspaper-reading can be a habit or indicative of spontaneous engagement. There is evidence that media use is often habitual, ritualistic and unselective (Barwise & Ehrenberg, 1988).

If audiences are viewed as having unlimited freedom, without taking into account the context within which media use takes place—the social setting—it could be argued that this is "runaway" individualism. Reimer (1998:137) believes this completely ignores the notion of contextualization. An individual exists in a particular milieu that makes certain requirements, has behavioral expectations, and roles could dictate media choice more than other factors.

Some critics note that "uses and gratifications" theory offers insufficient understanding of the link between individual psychological needs and the influence of cultural/social contexts on media use and interpretation (Grossberg, Wartella & Whitney, 1998). They claim it fails to see the individual as a complicated being, whose needs at a given moment are coupled with his social situation and membership in a group. They believe that it ignores the social background of communications and civilization as a system of shared meanings.

As a theoretical stance, critics say "uses and gratifications" theory foregrounds individual psychological and personality factors and backgrounds sociological interpretations. Morley (1992) acknowledges that individual differences in interpretation do exist, but he stresses the importance of subcultural socio-economic differences in shaping the ways in which people interpret their experiences (via shared "cultural codes").

"Uses and gratifications" theorists (e.g., Morley, 1992) tend to exaggerate active and conscious choice, whereas media can be forced on some people rather than chosen freely. This stance can also lead to the exaggeration of openness of interpretation, implying that audiences may obtain almost any kind of gratification regardless of content or of "preferred readings."

Its functionalist emphasis is viewed by some critics as politically conservative: if proponents insist that people will always find some gratifications from any use of media, they may adopt a complacently uncritical stance towards what the mass media currently offer (Webster, 1998).

While the critical studies area presents a challenge to "uses and gratifications" theory, it is very much outside the realm of this investigation, since subjects are not asked to assign meanings to text messages. The use and frequency of newspaper readers' efforts is under study, using standard statistical techniques, not the meaning readers attach to the newspaper.

In using a functionalist approach in spite of its limitations, the researcher does not take issue with current trends in semiotics and the assignment of meaning to media messages. It could be argued that a person in a religious sub-culture does assign different meanings to the material put forth by journalists each day, but this is not a study in interpretation of the media. Its goal is more to ascertain a link between media behavior and religious identity. The text, meaning and symbols are clearly the study of other investigations.

3.10 SUMMARY

"Uses and gratifications" theory is used to explain the roadmap, why particular consumers chose specific media publications, guided by religious preference and degree of involvement. As to why this is preferred to a critical studies approach, the emphasis is on behavior not on interpretation of media. It is an attempt to find a link between religious behavior, not philosophy, and actions in the everyday world, such as newspaper readership.

While this book focuses on newspapers, many research findings from the Internet and newer communications vehicles are transferable. Since ritualized contact in closed communities focuses on face-to-face meetings at services, news could be interpreted through conversation and one could expect less need for columnists' analysis or chatroom discussion.

Chapter Four

Research Design and Methodology

4.1 INTRODUCTION

Based on the theories discussed in Chapters 2 and 3, the idea evolved to investigate these concepts' relevance to understanding the relationship between religious impulses and newspaper use. While characteristics such as age, education and income have been studied for newspaper reading patterns, religious denominational preferences and degree of adherence to a set of religious principles have been less investigated (Buddenbaum: 1992, 1994).

This research was undertaken with a heuristic emphasis (Kerlinger, 1986:8), seeking to discover new interpretations and shed new light on an existent web of theories. As a heuristic rather than predictive study, this book seeks to uncover linkages that could be tested in the future under more stringent conditions, perhaps with a larger number of respondent groups.

Heuristic research is problem-solving, but the emphasis is on imaginative and not routine matters, with the goal of revealing interrelationships rather than of establishing general laws. While prediction is an important aspect of theory-based research, research can also be phenomenological; seeking to uncover specific relations and develop a deeper understanding of constructs that move in tandem with one another, without spawning mathematical equations or formulaic rules.

4.2 LINK WITH THEORIES UNDER INVESTIGATION

"Community ties" and "secularization" theories are used to understand religiosity (Chapter 2). Respondents could be in a majority religion or minority faith and have varying degrees of observance. This research design allows for measurement of belief and behavior whatever the type of religious community. It makes concrete many of the constructs expressed in the theories.

"Social identity" theory (Tajfel, 1981) is closely linked to issues of ingroup identification. "Social identity" theory posits that threats to group identity, which minorities experience more in a multicultural society (compared to larger, plurality groups), should increase ingroup identification (Worchel & Coutant, 1998). The overall research design is intended to gauge whether the two groups that are religious, cultural minorities in the USA (Mormons and Orthodox Jews) will have higher ingroup identification levels than a mainstream Protestant group (Methodists) and have different newspaper purchase/ use patterns.

4.3 OVERVIEW OF RESEARCH AND LINK WITH RESEARCH PROBLEM

The research problem under investigation is whether insular religious minority communities have different newspaper use patterns from the broader society, and how this might be explained. The first step was to develop hypotheses (Chapter 1), followed by a questionnaire, administered at churches and temples of three denominations: Mormon and Orthodox Jewish (representing minorities) and Methodist (representing average USA citizens).

The hypotheses used in this study are designed to give guiding power. Without specific hypotheses, the problem would have been too vague and the research direction unclear. In terms of this study, specific hypotheses (Section 1.8) were posited about the relationships among religiosity, ingroup identification and newspaper use.

However, given the threats to internal and external validity inherent in the research design (Kerlinger, 1986), no claim is made of generalizability to an entire denomination. Rather, a "snapshot" is being taken of members of three religious groups at a particular place and time.

4.4 THE QUESTIONNAIRE

An 81–question paper and pencil self-report instrument questionnaire was developed with demographic categories (e.g., education, income), which could be subject to standard statistical procedures. The questionnaire was designed to operationalize constructs that existed hitherto primarily as conceptual definitions. Questions were grouped into scales (groupings of related questions representing the constructs). At times, questions were phrased in the negative, requiring reverse-scoring to avoid a respondent mindset that gives routine answers to all questions without much thought.

The scales are labeled: 1) religiosity; 2) ingroup identification; 3) newspaper use; 4) political/civic participation; 5) fundamentalism; 6) conservatism; 7) news trust.

A pilot study was undertaken, with clergy filling out initial draft questionnaires to ensure that the wording of questions would be understandable to adherents of each of the three faiths. Following that, 210 completed questionnaires were obtained, divided equally between the three faiths. Statistical data analyses followed, relying primarily on the Principal Components method of factor reduction, building scales from individual questions. Factors were then analyzed, seeking confirmation or rejection of hypotheses.

Each of the seven constructs was based on a four-to-eight question scale in the survey instrument, and these were expected to produce cohesive factor rotation loadings.

4.4.1 Religiosity

Religiosity as a construct needs to be distinguished from religion (type): Mormon, Methodist or Jew. Religiosity refers to degree of observance or intensity of belief.

Primary indicators of degree of religiosity are attending services, praying privately or reading Scriptures on one's own. An individual who scores high on the religiosity scale is apt to attend services several times a week and engage in religious activities independently. An individual who scores low on the religiosity scale may attend services only several times a year and may not structure leisure-time around religious activities, whether in private or with a group.

Some examples of Likert-scale statements probing religiosity were "The religious quest is an essential part of my life," "The principles of my religious faith serve as guidelines for my actions," or a negative response to "I doubt the existence of God."

4.4.2 Ingroup Identification

This construct is included to determine whether the respondent shows marked preference for one's group, as a sign of ingroup identification, and a preference for action if group interests are threatened. An individual who scores high on the ingroup identification scale socializes primarily with others in his faith, is strongly loyal to the faith above the broader society, and supports ingroup marriage. An individual who scores low on the ingroup identification scale has broader social ties and is perhaps equally at home in all cultures.

This construct was measured through response to Likert-scale statements such as "I am willing to take action if the interests of my religious group are threatened," "The best friends are those that share your religion," or "I am against children from my faith marrying persons not in my religion."

4.4.3 Newspaper Use

Berelson (1949) conducted a study in New York City during a newspaper strike that became a widely-cited model toward understanding what the newspaper means to different people. In this study, his approach was followed closely, and every attempt was made to use the same categories. Many of his questions were used in developing the constructs. Berelson described five ways people used the newspaper:

- For "respite" or recreation, (using the newspaper to unwind from stress, a tension-reliever) measured by responses on questions such as "I relax when I read the newspaper";
- For "public affairs," (using the newspaper to develop opinions)," measured by high ratings on statements such as "I read the editorial page of the newspaper";
- For "information," (using the newspaper to be knowledgeable about what is going on in the community), measured by response to statements such as "I read the newspaper to be informed about political issues";
- For "entertainment," (using the newspaper either for pleasure or to find out about pleasurable activities), measured by response to statements such as "I find out about what is at the movies by reading the newspaper";
- For "socialization," (using the newspaper to feel joined to others beyond the family or block in the broader community), measured by response to statements such as "I feel connected to important people through the newspaper."

4.4.4 Political/Civic Participation

The construct of political/civic participation is used in this research to refer to joining community boards, going to hearings, participating in organizations and activities. An individual who scores high in political/civic participation joins many organizations in the community and is apt to devote much leisure-time to neighborhood organizations; an individual low in political/civic participation is apt to decline from group activities and spend more leisure time on alone or with family.

Some statements which gauged political/civic participation were "(I) go to meetings about civic issues," "(I) contribute money or time to political parties," or "(I) attend political events."

4.4.5 Religious Fundamentalism

Religious fundamentalism is an unerring belief in the literacy of the Bible (Dollar, 1973:5). A person who scores high on the religious fundamentalism scale believes that the Bible is literally true, compared to a more figurative, literary, or metaphorical interpretation. A person who scores low on the fundamentalism scale reads Scripture with more literary license and may believe in a more folkloric interpretation (Section 2.5.1).

Agreement with statements such as "Every word of the Bible is true" was seen as reflective of a high degree of fundamentalism. Jews consider the Bible to be the Five Books of Moses or Old Testament (Heilman & Cohen, 1989); Mormons and Methodists view the Bible as the Old Testament and the New Testament (Ostling, 1999). Each group interpreted the statement according to its definition of the Bible, but this did not seem problematic, as either way it addressed a literal versus expansive or metaphoric interpretation.

4.4.6 Conservatism

The construct of conservatism addresses issues such as the role of Government, opinions on abortion and states' rights in the USA. Conservatives in the USA are against "big Government" in favor of increased local control and against abortion. Hence, groups such as the "Moral Majority" demand legislation that would outlaw abortion and give more rights to the states over federal government. An individual who scores high on conservatism scales supports more local control versus federal governmental controls; an individual who scores low on conservatism scales (considered a "liberal") hoLds the opposite views. Statements such as "The USA is under God's protection," or "The President's authority comes from God," were presented as gauges of conservatism.

4.4.7 News Trust

The concept of news trust examines respondents' relative belief in the factuality of the newspaper and reporters' judgments above news gained from the grapevine in religious communities. An individual who scores high on the news trust scale favors reporters' interpretation of the news; a person who scores low on the news trust scale prefers to get news from religious publications and interpretation by religious officiants and friends in the community.

Agreement with statements such as "News about my religious group is bi-ased in the secular newspaper" is a gauge of news trust. Other statements in-cluded were: "My main source of news is friends in my religious commu-nity," and "I trust my clergyman's analysis of world/national news events more than what is reported in secular newspapers."

4.5 SELECTION OF SCALE TYPE

Kerlinger (1986:453) notes that there are three major types of attitude scales: summated rating scales, equal-appearing interval scales and cumulative (or Guttman) scales.

A summated rating scale (one type of which is called a Likert-type scale) is a set of attitude items, all of which are considered of approximately equal "attitude value," and to each of which subjects respond with degrees of agree-ment or disagreement (intensity). The scores of the items of such a scale are summed, or summed and averaged, to yield an individual's attitude score. As in all attitude scales, the purpose of the summated rating scale is to place an individual somewhere on an agreement continuum of the attitude in question.

If a construct involves several questions, the "average of averages" is taken for each respondent's answer to create a composite statistic for the "con-struct" under investigation. For example, if a respondent scored 4.2 on a 5–point Likert-scale on "fundamentalism," it meant that her worldview was deeply fundamentalist and totality of the "average of averages" was impor-tant than her responses to individual statements such as "every word of the Bible is true" in her mind and "the USA is under God's protection."

A summated (Likert) rating scale was chosen by the researcher since it allows for the intensity of attitude expression. Subjects can agree or agree strongly. When there are five or seven possible categories of response, it is obvious that the response variance should be greater than with only two or three categories, such as "agree," "disagree," or "no opinion" (Kerlinger, 1986:454). Each component of a Likert-scale questionnaire is presumed to have equal value.

The second choice Kerlinger (1986:454) is the "equal-appearing interval scale," which is built on different principles. Each item is assigned a scale value; the value of each statement is not equal. The items of the final scale are so selected that the intervals between them are equal, an important and desir-able psychometric feature.

Kerlinger (1986:455) defines the cumulative or Guttman scale as consist-ing of a relatively small set of homogeneous items that are unidimensional. This scale is often used in intelligence testing. It makes the assumption, for instance, that if a child gets a question right at a certain level of difficulty, he will have answered correctly all questions below that level, obviating the need for testing.

Having selected the Likert-scale statements, intensity of agreement or disagreement, it became possible to select factor analysis as the primary statistical technique for the study. Factor analysis depends upon similarly-weighted items in scales which comprise the factor. The selection of this technique, rather than the other two types of scales, made it possible to proceed in an orderly fashion and draw correlations between sets of variables.

4.6 THE POPULATION

4.6.1 Selection of the Groups

Two groups were chosen to represent the minority population: Orthodox Jews and Mormons. To represent the majority Protestant culture, Methodists were chosen.

The results of this study are not generalizable to other groups of Orthodox Jews and Mormons in the USA or world. This is descriptive research and applies only to Westchester County, New York.

The Mormon and Orthodox Jewish groups were chosen as representatives of insular religious minorities since, in order to fulfill many of their own religious requirements, they must isolate themselves to some degree from the American mainstream. The Mormon faith, for example, requires a full day restraint from work, shopping and competitive sports on the (Sunday) Sabbath. Prohibitions against caffeine (including soft drinks) and alcohol make some members self-conscious at secular-sponsored social events (Ostling, 1999).

Orthodox Jews observe full-day (Saturday) Sabbath periods, with restraint from working and various recreational activities. For example, on the Sabbath one cannot spend money to go to a movie or athletic event (Heilman & Cohen, 1989). Kosher dietary laws prohibit eating, among other things, pork, shellfish and meats from improperly slaughtered animals (Heilman & Cohen, 1989; Rushkoff, 2003). The Methodist, mainstream Protestant group, has less rigid rules that might lead to insular behavior.

4.6.2 Selection of the Survey Site

Westchester County, an affluent New York City suburb with a population of about 925,000, was chosen as the site of the study (Westchester County Planning Department, 2003). Westchester County is adjacent to the largest USA city and commercial hub of the nation and has a variety of religious groups.

The New York City metropolitan area provides a rich mixture of religious, ethnic and racial groups, including many recent immigrants. As a major port, it has been the historical focus of immigration into the United States over the past century.

4.6.2.1 *Jews*

There are between 90,000 and 100,000 Jews in Westchester County. Approximately, 50% affiliate with temples; 50% do not. Of the 45,000 to 50,000 affiliated Jews, approximately 6,000 belong to Orthodox Temples, the most observant branch of Judaism. Orthodox Jews are about 6% of Jews in Westchester; nationwide, Orthodox Jews are 10% of all Jews. (Westchester Jewish Conference Research Department, 2003). Jews (Orthodox and non-Orthodox) constitute 2–3% of the USA population (American Jewish Congress Research Department, 2003).

Orthodox Jews were chosen for the survey because they are the most observant, easy to measure in their numbers, and because they are always affiliated with a Temple in order to carry out religious mandates. They are indeed a religious minority even within the American Jewish community, so their outlook was deemed appropriate as an exemplar of minority status.

Two Orthodox Temples were chosen for administering the questionnaire: Young Israel Temple of Scarsdale and Young Israel Temple of White Plains. They are located within three miles of each other and expressing similar dogma, since they are joined loosely in an association of Young Israel Temples throughout the country.

4.6.2.2 *Mormons*

There are two Mormon Churches in Westchester County, with approximately 3,750 total members (Stern, 2003a). The Scarsdale Church in Central Westchester, rather than a counterpart in Northern Westchester, was chosen because it was close geographically to the two Central Westchester Temples and members thought to be more similar socioeconomically.

4.6.2.3 *Methodists*

Several Methodist churches were selected as sites for administering the survey. There are many Methodist churches in the county, but each of them has, on average, far fewer members than houses of worship in the other two religious groups.

Some Methodist services attract fewer than 40 adults on a given Sunday. Stern (2003:A1) notes that Methodist congregations of only a few dozen aging members have become common in Westchester County. More churches had to be visited to acquire the same number of questionnaires compared to the other faiths. Still, they are categorized as mainstream, in that their philosophy represents moderate Protestantism. It is a centrist approach, as Stern (2003:A1) characterizes the Methodist Church, that makes it a "bellwether" of Protestantism.

The number of United Methodist Church members in Westchester County is as follows (Southwick, 2003):

- 8,475 adult members, and
- 1,119 "preparatory" members (under adult age).

All of the Methodist Churches were within eight miles of each other and situated in Central Westchester.

4.7 THE SAMPLE

4.7.1 Sampling and Randomness

Kerlinger (1986) discusses randomness and the law of large numbers as pivotal in statistical analyses designed to produce generalizable findings. Different laws, however, exist for randomized groups and correlated groups, which make up the sample of this study. Since no attempt is made to generalize once randomness is unavailable, different statistical principles apply.

The respondents in the three religious denominations are in correlated groups, where relationships are suggested between behavioral constructs, but are not proven with the same intensity and generalizability as in randomized groups (Kerlinger, 1986:179).

Untrained observers come to certain conclusions about other people and the environment. While they may do so based on personal experience, researchers must scientifically investigate and measure the "experiences" of other people, beyond friends and neighbors, to draw valid conclusions (Kerlinger, 1986:109). Otherwise, the evidence is merely "anecdotal."

It was not possible to take a true random sample of each religious group: clergy in the post-9-11 atmosphere were not willing to release a written list of congregants from which to probe religious opinions.

However, clergy were willing to allow the author access to respondents after services, at fellowship hours, and at nighttime events. Congregants were encouraged to participate by the clergy at each event, but not all attendees participated.

4.7.2 Classification of Samples

4.7.2.1 Probability and Nonprobability Samples

Probability samples use some form of random sampling in one or more of their stages (Kerlinger, 1986:119–120). Nonprobability samples do not use random sampling. There are three types:

* Quota sampling—in which knowledge of strata of the population is used to select sample members, who are representative or "typical." It is commonly used in public opinion polls;
* Purposive—characterized by use of judgment and deliberate effort to obtain representative samples by including presumably typical areas or groups in the sample;
* Accidental—weakest, includes methods such as treating a college class as a sample for reasons of convenience.

This study relies on "purposive" sampling. With randomness unavailable, nonprobability rules were in effect. Groups were chosen "on purpose" rather than "by accident." These were groups that were thought to demonstrate enough contrast with one another to facilitate the aims of the research—the study of what were predicted to be behavioral differences between insular religious minorities and majority religious group members.

4.7.3 Contacting Clergy

The clergy of each congregation were contacted and shown a copy of the questionnaire. This step was taken so that each officiant could screen out language that did not apply to the unique faith.

For example, a local rabbi told this author that the proper name for Jewish membership fees is "dues"; and all Jewish questionnaires used that term henceforth. A Mormon officiant told the researcher that the correct name for membership fees is "tithes"; and all Mormon survey instruments bore that appellation on question #26 thereafter. A Methodist minister told the researcher that the correct appellation was "pledges" for the yearly fee; and all Methodist questionnaires were so emended.

That was the only item that had to be emended to reflect different religious groups' terminology.

4.8 DATA COLLECTION PROCESS

The survey project had three phases: the first was to obtain permission and cooperation from the various groups and clergy; the second was the pilot study; the third, conducting the actual study.

After obtaining permission from clergy in each group, the researcher administered 106 questionnaires at one site from each religious group, with participants attending a worship service or evening community event as part of the pilot study.

The Mormons and Methodists allow writing instruments to be used on the Sabbath in church; hence, the questionnaire administration took place directly after the Sunday service, at fellowship hours or in mandatory religious education classes. Orthodox Jews are not allowed to write in the Temple on the Sabbath (Heilman & Cohen, 1989). Therefore, the questionnaires were administered at evening events after sundown on Saturday and Sunday nights.

The pilot study allowed the researcher to set up computer programs, databases and make sure that the research techniques could be effectuated. It was used to check the accuracy of scales, make sure questions "load" together in factors, combinations of questions useful for statistical analysis. The visits with clergy helped to check instrumentation for terminology errors that could affect accuracy.

4.9 SELECTION OF METHOD FOR RESPONDENT CONTACT

Surveys can be classified by the following methods of obtaining information: personal interview, mail questionnaire, panel and telephone (Kerlinger, 1986:378).

A personal interview was rejected as a potential technique since it would have introduced an element of researcher bias, with respondents perhaps tempted through heightened social interaction to offer answers that they believed the researcher wished to hear (Kerlinger, 1986). By approaching the respondents with a written survey, interaction was minimal; all respondents had a uniform set of questions in front of them. In practice, they could have asked the researcher for an explanation of questions, but few respondents asked to have questions explained.

Mailing questionnaires was considered but rejected as possibly yielding a low response rate in a time of heightened security in the USA and suspicion of strangers' posing questions about religious beliefs.

The panel technique was not under consideration, since respondents could be influenced too heavily by one another's opinion. It is used in the USA more frequently for consumer focus groups where discussion with the moderator is considered a positive aspect (Kerlinger, 1986).

The telephone interview technique was not under consideration since none of the denominations would release telephone or address lists.

The in-person questionnaire was selected since it was believed to yield the highest response rate and allow development of Likert-type quantitative scales.

4.10 RESULTS OF THE PILOT STUDY

The pilot study results did not require the researcher to make any changes in operating procedure. The 70 respondents from each group completed the questionnaire at the following sites during November/December 2002 and January/March 2003:

Table 4.   Sites and Events with Dates Where Survey Was Administered

Site	Event & Date	Total Surveys		
		Jewish	*Methodist*	*Mormon*
Orthodox Temple #1	Political speaker on Israel, 11/3/02	27		
Methodist Church #1	Fellowship hour after services, 11/17/02		9	
Mormon Church #1	Education class after services, 12/22/02			70
Orthodox Temple #1	Art auction, 1/25/03	22		
Methodist Church #2	Fellowship hour after services, 1/26/03		12	
Methodist Church #3	Fellowship hour after services, 2/9/03		22	
Methodist Church #4	Fellowship hour after services, 2/23/03		9	
Methodist Church #5	Fellowship hour after services, 3/02/03		8	
Methodist Church #6	Fellowship hour after services, 3/9/03		10	
Orthodox Temple #2	Visiting guest rabbi lecture, 2/9/03	21		
Sum by denomination		70	70	70

4.11 THREATS TO VALIDITY IN THE STUDY

4.11.1 Post-Hoc Fallacy

Kerlinger (1986:348) notes that one of the dangers of this type of study is the *post-hoc* fallacy—assigning causes to phenomena that are related but not causal, while they may occur sequentially. The fallacy derives from the error in logic of arguing, *"post hoc, propter hoc"*—"after this, therefore by reason of this." A classic example is: "I said my prayers before sunrise, therefore the sun rose." This *post-hoc* fallacy is particularly prevalent in research designed to establish a "connection" rather than prove a generalizable theory through randomized groups.

Applying to this study, members of a particular house of worship may exhibit certain traits or behave in specific ways. It is important to remember that respondents have selected a particular house of worship for a reason which may extend beyond spiritual conviction. For example, a particular social class may attend a certain church in a community, since co-religionists share common habits of dress, income and spending level. They feel comfortable sitting among their peers.

They may go to church many times per week and exhibit signs of increased religiosity, more than attendees at other churches where there is more diversity, but the increased attendance could be due to increased comfort level and shared social class. A *post-hoc* fallacy would be to say that a group (e.g., Methodist Church #2) is more religiously observant then Methodist Church #3 and motivated, in that they attend church more frequently, when in fact they came in with shared characteristics that prompted higher attendance.

4.11.2 Problems with Self-Selection in a Non-Experimental Study

In an experimental study, greater controls exist regarding variables and assignment of subjects. In an experimental research design, it is hypothesized that if X happens, then Y results. One then observes Y to see if concomitant variation happens, giving scientific evidence of "if X, then Y." The researcher can manipulate X in the laboratory and observe Y increase or decrease. Operant conditioning experiments offer a good example: if food is offered, the Pavlovian dog salivates, according to a stimulus-response model. If food—the independent variable—is withdrawn, salivation disappears (Kerlinger, 1986:348–349).

In non-experimental research, on the other hand, y is observed and an X or several X's are also observed, before, after, or concomitant to the observation of y. It could be argued that the same logic and goals are present in both forms of research: to establish validity of so-called conditional statements. The essential difference is that in non-experimental research, X cannot be manipulated as an independent variable. Subjects in this study cannot be assigned by the researcher to another religion, for example, to ensure that all groups had an equal number of subjects by race or education level, as they could in a laboratory experiment.

In non-experimental design, a situation could materialize where an imbalance in race, education or income creates a desired effect, rather than the variable being studied. Respondents may self-select homogeneous groupings, unconsciously creating new conditions which flaw the research; an experimental situation controls for extraneous variables by allowing the researcher to balance groups according to certain criteria (e.g. race, income).

In terms of this study, could self-selection have created non-equivalent groups? In the case of Orthodox Jews, most Orthodox Jews are born into Orthodox households, so selecting a house of worship based on income or occupation would be highly unlikely. In addition, they are not allowed to ride in a motorized vehicle to the temple on the Sabbath; and so the temple must be within walking distance (Heilman & Cohen, 1989). Therefore one could not speculate that a decision was made to affiliate based on socioeconomic factors that make the results inaccurate. Since there are only two Mormon churches in the county and they are forty minutes' drive apart, again one has little choice in where to worship, and self-selection by factors (e.g., occupation, income) could not come into play in determining who attends the temple. Methodists would have more choices based on social class and comfort, due to the larger number of churches in Westchester County.

4.11.3 Non-Respondent Bias

Sometimes there are differences that bias the results in a "survey-decline rate," a refusal rate, among people who otherwise share common characteristics. This is known as "non-respondent bias" (Kerlinger, 1986). Simply put: the people who did not respond in a survey might have responded in an entirely different fashion from those who did respond. The reasons, entirely undiscoverable to the researcher, might range from objection to the instrument to temporary psychological or physical discomforts, such as needing to care for a sick child or visit the latrine.

It is unknown whether there was a differential survey decline rate among those less interested in religion and taking the time to answers the questions, since there was no way to survey the respondents who declined to answer, for example, at a church fellowship hour.

The researcher approached congregants and, after the clergyman had encouraged participation in services, asked them to complete the questionnaire, which took about 12 minutes on average. Those people who were more interested in talking about other subjects with their peers, perhaps, were less inclined to take time out for the research. More talkative individuals, for example, could have been more apt to bypass abstain the questionnaire in order to converse more, creating a bias in terms of quieter individuals. Alternatively, those individuals who felt more positively about their religion could have been more apt to complete the questionnaire than non-respondents. However, as a rough estimate, the researcher found that not more than about 5% declined to participate.

4.11.4 External Validity and Generalizability

No attempt is made to generalize these survey results to broader populations because the group of respondents is neither randomized nor claimed to be representative of larger populations.

4.12 FACTOR ANALYSIS AND IDENTIFICATION OF FINAL CONSTRUCTS

Factor analysis was used to create scales of religiosity, ingroup identification, newspaper use and political outlook, with each scale having several subscales (Table 5). By combining questions to create scales with close correlations, having a Cronbach's alpha of at least 0.7, condensation occurs into solitary constructs called "factors" (Dillon & Goldstein, 1984). While it may be possible to analyze individual questions, the richness that results by combining questions under expressive semantic labels makes it possible for both the researcher and her audience to decipher complex data.

The interpretation of data can be viewed as much as an art as a science. When four or five questions coalesce to represent a single concept (e.g. religiosity or ingroup identification), the beauty of higher math comes into play and an aesthetic presentation is possible that is more complete than it would have otherwise been.

4.13 PRINCIPAL COMPONENTS FACTOR ANALYSIS

Dillon & Goldstein (1984:20) note that two types of factor analysis exist: "principal components" (PC); and, the "common factor" analytic model.

"Principal components" analysis is "a data reduction technique where the primary goal is to construct linear combinations of the original variables that account for as much of the [original] total variation as possible. The successive linear combinations are extracted in such a way that they are uncorrelated with each other and account for successively smaller amounts of the total variation."

The "common factor" analytic model is also a data reduction technique, with the main difference that interest is focused on the part of the total variation that a particular variable shares with the other variables constituting the set.

The "principal components" method of factor analysis is used in this study. For example, religiosity is extracted as a "principal component" of the variance, explaining the statistical relationship among all the variables.

It was also believed that the "principal components" method of extraction would "tease" out responses about trust in clergy, friends, and religious communities' interpretation of the news, but that proved to be the weakest set of constructs in the study and did not materialize or result in groups of questions that "loaded" together with similar responses (see Appendix B). That is not a shortcoming of the Principal Component factor analysis method but rather a reflection of the diffuse nature of information dissemination and flow in the New York area and the relative assimilation of religious individuals in the secular world, where news discussion is not limited to the religious community.

4.14 DATA REDUCTION

This research involved conducting two rounds of factor analysis. It produced the principal components, which is the function of any data set reduction. This method of simplification makes understanding possible.

The purpose of the first round was to group together questions with similar responses which loaded together to create scales. By creating scales, the vast amount of data generated from 81 questions is now reduced to a workable number of constructs. When hypotheses are first formed, there is often very little theory to rely on, and a hit-or-miss strategy exists regarding collection of data (Dillon & Goldstein, 1984:23). Questions are generated that are believed to produce similar constellations of responses, but a researcher is not sure. One could presume, for example, that someone who reads Scripture on his own as a measure of religiosity also would response positively to the statement, "I pray privately or meditate," but it is unknown. By performing a Principal Component factor analysis around the subject of religiosity, and finding means on these questions moving in tandem, the researcher feels confident that a correlation exists and a scale can be constructed for further cross-correlations around the theme of religiosity. It could then be determined, for example, if it correlated with another construct (set of questions) organized around the theme of informational use of the newspaper.

Instead of analyzing individual questions and addressing 81 individual areas, a uniform construct labeled "religiosity" now exists. The researcher can then determine if individuals high in private expressions of religiosity use the newspaper more for information; rather, they might ignore the newspaper as an informational tool and have another use for it—as an example, for respite, escape from worldly matters.

The scales, since they combine individual questions, could later be used in figuring out descriptive statistics, norms, standard deviations, but their purpose is 1) data-reduction and 2) ascertaining mathematically that questions that were hitherto intuitively linked actually share joint numerical "loadings." Respondents who give high or low ratings on certain issues are expected to give corresponding answers on other similar questions.

4.14.1 Item Grouping in First Factor Analysis

As a result of the factor analysis, groupings of similar questions emerged that shared common loadings over 0.3. Out of these loadings, questions were evaluated and given expressive semantic labels as scales, based on groups of questions that statistically hung together. Since many of the scales, such as religiosity and ingroup identification, included many more questions than the other scales, they were broken down into sub-scales, using the same statistical methods used to create the main scale.

The goal at this point in the data analysis was to eliminate unreliable, cross-loaded or uncorrelated items that detracted from or contributed little to the statistical and conceptual integrity of the questionnaire and its component factors. Items were subject to elimination (but were not necessarily eliminated) if they displayed one of or a combination of the following characteristics:

- Detraction from a factor's reliability (alpha),
- A small value for the measure of sampling adequacy (usually < 0.07),
- A factor loading of less than 0.30,
- A cross-loading on three or more factors,
- A cross-loading on two items if the loadings were nearly equal.

Of the 81 original questions, 30 exhibited statistically cohesive groupings and were afforded semantic labels that expressed the common construct.

Thirty questions were now grouped into the first factors; a pool of 51 questions remained. The same criteria were applied as in the first factor analysis:

Table 5.   Twelve Factors Categorized by Sub-Topics

Broader Categorization		Factor Sub-groupings
Religiosity	1	Comfort/Security
	2	Time-commitment
	3	Spiritual quest
Ingroup identification	1	Stalwart defender
	2	Friendship
	3	Pride and bonding
Newspaper use	1	Public affairs
	2	Respite
	3	Socialization
	4	Entertainment
Political stance	1	Political/civic participation
	2	Conservatism/fundamentalism

questions were removed that did not "load" into groupings of three questions or more; questions were removed from scales that coalesced, but their removal boosted the alpha ratings. Scales with an alpha below 0.7 were not considered powerful enough to warrant further study, even if they comprised more than three questions which "loaded" together.

These 51 items converged into five cohesive factors, and each was given a semantically expressive label. Twenty-six questions did not "load" into significant groupings of three or more questions and they were dropped from the survey (See Appendix C for a list of dropped questions).

4.14.2 Making up the Factors from the Original Seven Constructs

Six of the original seven constructs are represented in the final 12 scales. Therefore it was concluded that six original constructs had been upheld as being present: religiosity, ingroup identification, newspaper use, political/civic participation, conservatism, fundamentalism. The seventh original construct was "news trust," but questions failed to load together in the Principal Components analysis. Some of the larger scales were broken down later into sub-groupings.

Given this, the decision was made to use 12 factors in further analytical procedures, which include the sub-scales.

4.15 SUMMARY OF EACH FACTOR

Having examined the categorization of factors, by topic, here is the list of factors as they emerged in terms of their power.

Table 6.   Factors As They Emerged

Factor #	Factor Label
1	Religion as comfort/security
2	Religion as time-commitment
3	Newspaper use: information and public affairs
4	Political/civic participation
5	Newspaper use: respite
6	Ingroup identification: stalwart defender
7	Newspaper use: socialization
8	Religion as spiritual quest
9	Ingroup identification: friendship
10	Newspaper use: entertainment
11	Ingroup identification: pride and bonding
12	Conservatism/fundamentalism

Religion, a universal need, can be broken down into subcomponents. A person can use it to take comfort in hard times and find security (the intent of this constellation of questions), as a social time-commitment or to obtain spiritual enhancement. This factor reflects the need to live in a more fixed universe, praying when chaos becomes rampant, and believing the country is under God's care as a way of attaining security.

Many people use religious activities as a leisure time-commitment in their lives outside of work. This factor reflects an emphasis on activities and doing, rather than inner spirituality. This factor reflects free-time involvement in religious education, social activities at the house of worship, governance and leadership. For people who score highly on this scale, religion is perhaps their largest time-commitment outside of work.

A constellation of similar responses exists around the concept of missing the newspaper when it is absent, making it an important part of one's routine, like hygiene or tooth-brushing. Connected are habits such as reading most

Table 7.   Factor 1—Religion as Comfort/Security

Factor 1 Religion as Comfort/Security (n = 183)				
Mean = 3.99	Standard Deviation = 3.18	Min. = 3.21	Max. = 4.4	Reliability (alpha) = 0.77

Question Number and Content
7   I find comfort in my religion during difficult times.
14   My religious faith is a major source of security in my life.
23   I pray privately or meditate.
79   The USA is under God's protection.

Table 8.   Factor 2—Religion as Time-Commitment

		Factor 2		
		Religion as Time Commitment (n = 193)		
Mean =	*Standard Deviation =*	*Min. =*	*Max. =*	*Reliability (alpha) =*
3.59	4.21	3.18	3.9	0.85

Question Number and Content

18	During my free time I am mostly involved with activities from my religious group.
24	I attend religious education activities.
25	I attend social activities from congregation.
27	I read magazines and religious publications from group.
29	I cooperate with most decisions made by leaders at my house of worship.

news in text format, including the Internet and magazines, and liking particular columnists. Connected is dependence on the printed news page for information on which to base financial decisions and develop an editorial stance.

The constructs of public affairs use (opinion formation) and information attainment are combined in one unified factor, compared to the original Berelson study (1949), which separated the two concepts. While the original concepts' methodology first used in this study was meant to parallel Berelson, when actual results came in it was apparent from the factor loadings that readers do not distinguish today between the two functions in contemporary life, but group them together under "information and public affairs."

The political/civic participation factor reflects attendance at meetings, civic events and donating money to important causes. The statements that

Table 9.   Factor 3—Newspaper Use: Information

		Factor 3		
		Newspaper Use: Information (n = 193)		
Mean =	*Standard Deviation =*	*Min. =*	*Max. =*	*Reliability (alpha) =*
3.3	7.82	2.54	3.99	0.88

Question Number and Content

38	I read a newspaper from my local community or metropolitan area.
39	Missing the newspaper makes me feel disconnected from the outside world.
40	Reading the newspaper every morning is part of my routine.
41	If what I read in the newspaper is discordant with teachings of my religion I read it anyway.
42	I read most of my news in text format, either in the newspaper or on the Internet.
46	I have my favorite newspaper columnists.
50	I find out about stocks or business concerns in the newspaper.
52	I read the editorial page of the newspaper.

Table 10.   Factor 4—Political/Civic Participation

Factor 4 Political/Civic Participation (n = 194)				
Mean = 2.31	Standard Deviation = 3.71	Min. = 2.15	Max. = 2.68	Reliability (alpha) = 0.81

Question Number and Content
32   I go to meetings about civic issues.
33   I contribute money or time to political parties.
36   I attend political events.

contributed to this factor were developed to probe the linkage between high levels of political participation/community involvement paralleling newspaper and religious commitments. Traditional theory hoLds that the same people are involved in all aspects of community life, as "joiners." The same people go to church to see fellow-citizens of the town, attend meetings, serve on boards and use the newspaper to stay abreast of these activities. Other people, by comparison, are "isolates," and shy away from all of these behaviors simultaneously.

Reading the newspaper is seen by many as a relaxing habit, removing one's mind from the problems of the day, one's livelihood. This factor unites data from responses regarding reliance on the newspaper to escape problems at hand.

Statements that coalesce to form this factor relate to in-group marriage, loyalty and acting in the group's self-interest. The "stalwart defender" label refers to being more loyal to one's religious community than to outside groups and a willingness to act defensively on behalf of the community.

This factor embodies reactions to statements about the social power of the newspaper. Many individuals use it as a tool to connect to others,

Table 11.   Factor 5—Newspaper Use: Respite

Factor 5 Newspaper Use: Respite (n = 198)				
Mean = 2.51	Standard Deviation = 2.95	Min. = 2.35	Max. = 2.72	Reliability (alpha) = 0.89

Question Number and Content
59   I escape from personal problems when I read the newspaper.
60   I escape from livelihood concerns when I read the newspaper.
61   I take my mind off other things when I read the newspaper.

Table 12.   Factor 6—Ingroup Identification: Stalwart Defender

Factor 6 Ingroup Identification: Stalwart Defender (n = 200)				
Mean = 3.68	*Standard Deviation =* 2.68	*Min. =* 3.14	*Max. =* 4.17	*Reliability (alpha) =* 0.68

Question Number and Content
15   I am against children from my faith marrying persons not in my religion.
12   I am more loyal to my religious group than to any other societal group.
17   I am willing to take action if the interests of my religious group are threatened.

particularly celebrities and those they consider prominent in the community. They read gossip columns—considered some of the "lighter" features in print journalism.

The most important question in this scale is the "religious quest" question and the whole approach to life based on religion. This indicates a "seeker" mentality, coupled with thinking about the existence of God and reading scripture on one's own. As compared to someone seeking religion for security (which indicates a holding on, tenacious view of life), the "questor" is driven to uncover spirituality whereever it can be found and to incorporate religious principles into all aspects of life.

Compared to other "ingroup identification" factors, this series of linked questions revolve around people limiting their friends and interactions outside the faith, choosing friends primarily from within. Perhaps this is to eliminate temptations from the outside world by keeping a tight circle of friendship (See Section 5.5).

This factor reflects motivation to research movie and television schedules by entertainment-oriented individuals through the newspaper, which they therefore find important to read. Even vacations can be planned in this manner. The lighter, feature side of news is emphasized by this group of questions.

Table 13.   Factor 7—Newspaper Use: Socialization

Factor 7 Newspaper Use: Socialization (n = 197)				
Mean = 2.12	*Standard Deviation =* 2.69	*Min. =* 2.03	*Max. =* 2.21	*Reliability (alpha) =* 0.74

Question Number and Content
63   I follow the lives of celebrities in the newspaper.
64   I feel connected to important people through the newspaper.
65   I read gossip/advice columns in the newspaper

Table 14.   Factor 8—Religion as Spiritual Quest

Factor 8 Religion as Spiritual Quest (n = 198)				
Mean =	Standard Deviation =	Min. =	Max. =	Reliability (alpha) =
4.2	0.74	3.49	4.69	0.85

Question Number and Content
1   Attending religious services regularly is important.
3   The religious quest is an essential part of my life.
6   My whole approach to life is based on my religion.
13   The principles of my religious faith serve as guidelines for my actions.
8   I doubt the existence of God.
28   I read Biblical teachings and scriptures on my own.
20   I believe that all religions are more or less the same.
21   Being a member of a church or synagogue is just a social custom for me.

This "ingroup identification" factor combines caring about what other people in the religious community think, identifying more with one's own group than the outside world, and giving others in the group, even financially. This factor differs from the "friendship" and the "stalwart defenders" labels because it reflects bonding to enjoy the give-and-take of being in a group, rather than keeping a hostile presence out by limiting friends. Those scoring high on this factor do not necessarily see the outside world as hostile toward their religion, but may rely more on internal close relationships for support.

This group of questions, when loaded into a single factor, consolidates conservative political views about abortion and expectations of high moral standards from elected public officials. This factor combines belief in a supreme being and the need for it to be reflected in moral behavior by public officials.

Table 15.   Factor 9—Ingroup Identification: Friendship

Factor 9 Ingroup Identification: Friendship (n = 196)				
Mean =	Standard Deviation =	Min. =	Max. =	Reliability (alpha) =
2.38	2.27	1.75	3.31	0.54

Question Number and Content
5   I believe that the best friends are those that share your religion.
19   I have many friends belonging to religions different from my own.
30   Interact with others outside my faith.

Table 16. Factor 10—Newspaper Use: Entertainment

Factor 10 *Newspaper Use: Entertainment (n = 195)*				
Mean = 277	*Standard Deviation =* 3.75	*Min. =* 1.82	*Max. =* 3.98	*Reliability (alpha) =* 0.67

Question Number and Content
48 I find out what is on television by reading the newspaper.
51 I plan vacations using the newspaper.
47 I find out what is at the movies by reading the newspaper.
38 I read a newspaper from my local community or metropolitan area.

Table 17. Factor 11—Ingroup Identification: Pride and Bonding

Factor 11 *Ingroup Identification: Pride and Bonding (n = 194)*				
Mean = 3.6	*Standard Deviation =* 3.18	*Min. =* 3.1	*Max. =* 4.27	*Reliability (alpha) =* 0.46

Question Number and Content
9 I care what members of my religious community think of me.
11 I feel proud when a member of my congregation excels or does something good.
10 I identify with my religious community more than the general society around me.
22 Members of my congregation have helped me through difficult times.
26 I contribute financially to my house of worship beyond required dues (tithes) (pledges).

4.16 CARRYOVER OF ORIGINAL CONCEPTS

The original constructs tested when the survey was designed were the following (see Appendix B). Each of the questions was designed to fit into one of these groupings, but not all the questions were used in creation of the factors:

- Religiosity (emerged as three subscales);
- Ingroup identification (emerged as three subscales);
- Political/civic participation (resulted in one factor);
- News-reading habits (addressed in categorical variables, probing subscription or non-subscription to newspaper, frequency of reading newspaper, rather than in factors based on continuous scales);
- "Uses and gratifications" (originally five in Berelson's seminal article; these translated into four factors, with public affairs and information combined into one);

• Conservatism/fundamentalism (resulted in one factor);
• News trust/analysis by clergy and community members (did not produce any factors).

The constructs relating to news trust did not hold up in the factor analysis and perhaps they were too diffuse in their intent. They were intended to rate faith in clergy's analysis of the news above the newspaper, as well as friends in the religious community interpreting the news for each other, in line with theories on the flow of information through social networks (Lazarsfeld, Katz & Gaudet, 1944).

The analysis of dropped questions (see Appendix C) shows the questions that did not survive factorial analysis. These questions had four sets of foci:

• Trusting clergy in their interpretation of world and local events,
• Trusting religious friends' interpretation of newspaper,
• Trusting/distrusting secular paper reporters,
• Finding evidence of news bias in secular papers.

These areas are certainly interesting to explore, with a wealth of possible information to generate, but require a more extensive study devoted exclusively to news trust. They did not link together sufficiently in this study to create even a unified factor, nor did they lead to any significant findings.

Table 18.   Factor 12—Conservatism/Fundamentalism

Factor 12 Conservatism/Fundamentalism (n = 196)				
Mean = 2.69	Standard Deviation = 3.6	Min. = 1.94	Max. = 3.32	Reliability (alpha) = 0.60

Question Number and Content
78   Every word of the Bible is true.
74   I think abortion should be outlawed.
80   Public officials should embody their religion's ethics.
81   The president's authority is derived from God.

4.17 SUMMARY

While many methodologies could have been used to investigate the link between newspaper use and religion (type), factor analysis allowed the greatest branching out to uncover religiosity motivation. By using a data-reduction technique like this, it was possible to uncover groups of questions that coalesced to form some of the most important findings of the study.

Chapter Five

Results and Discussion

5.1 INTRODUCTION

The purpose of this study is to determine whether insular religious communities (as represented by Mormons and Orthodox Jews) differ in their newspaper use/behavior from the mainstream Protestant population (represented by Methodist Church members). Hypotheses were generated initially to provide a launching ground for this investigation. The results of the hypothesis testing are reported in this chapter, in addition to other interesting results uncovered through an exploratory examination of data.

The results of this survey are limited to the groups investigated in Westchester County, New York in 2002–2003. The results cannot be generalized to the broader population.

Factor analysis allowed for data simplification, reducing the 81 questions in the survey to twelve manageable condensations of the constructs under investigation.

5.2 GENERAL CHARACTERISTICS OF THE GROUP SURVEYED

5.2.1 Descriptive Statistics of Each Group

The Methodist respondents were considerably older than the Jewish and Mormon respondents, with an average age of 55. The age of the average survey respondent was 46.

Women were represented more than men in the survey by almost a ⅔ ratio. There were differences between the three groups, with Mormons having the

Table 19.   Demographic Statistics on the Three Religious Groups

	Average Age	Married vs. Single		Male versus Female		Children Living Home— % Yes vs. No	
	Average Age	Married (%)	Single (%)	Male (%)	Female (%)	Children (Yes %)	Children Home (% No)
Mormon	36	52	48	45	55	40	60
Jewish	47	82	18	38	62	35	65
Methodist	55	51	41	24	76	24	76
Overall	46	63	37	36	64	59	41

most even distribution between men and women. Methodists were? female in composition.

In terms of marital status, 63% of all the respondents were married. Among Orthodox Jews, the highest percentage were married, compared to living in single-headed households: 82% to 18%.

In terms of total respondents, by an almost 60% to 40% margin, households included children still living at home. However, among Mormons, the youngest age group, that statistic was reversed. Perhaps many households consisted of couples who had not yet produced offspring. The Methodists, the eldest age group, also by a ? margin had no children in the household, perhaps having raised their children already.

5.2.2 The Overall Group as Readers and Media Users

Approximately 61% of the respondents read *The New York Times*, the major newspaper of the metropolitan area; 45% read *The Journal News*, the local paper for Westchester County; 24% read *The Wall Street Journal*, the principal business newspaper of the USA. Many respondents read several newspapers daily. 57% subscribe to a newspaper delivered at home or work, making it the most common means of obtaining it.

It is a highly literate, well-educated group with high incomes. 49% have attended or graduated college. A very large group, 41%, has postgraduate degrees. 27% have household incomes over $150,000. This is in line with the average income of Westchester Country, where the median single-home price in 2003 was $520,000 (Westchester County Planning Department, 2003).

Television use is not that important to respondents. 56% watch during the week "never to under two hours" daily. Radio use weekdays is "never to under two hours" (66%)daily which corresponds typically to commuting time to

Table 20. **Comparison of Newspaper Use Categorizations by Denomination**

| | Newspaper Use—Public Affairs (Factor #3) | | | Newspaper Use—Entertainment (Factor #10) | | |
	Mean	N	Std. Dev.	Mean	N	Std. Dev.
Jewish	3.63	66	0.72	3.10	67	1.00
Methodist	3.20	65	0.77	2.98	69	0.95
Mormon	2.69	62	0.78	2.50	61	0.92
Overall	3.19	201	0.85	2.88	197	0.99

| | Newspaper Use—Respite (Factor #5) | | | Newspaper Use—Socialization (Factor #7) | | |
	Mean	N	Std. Dev.	Mean	N	Std. Dev.
Jewish	2.93	69	0.91	2.12	69	1.01
Methodist	2.37	65	0.91	2.27	66	0.95
Mormon	2.16	63	1.04	2.01	61	0.87
Overall	2.50	197	1.00	2.14	196	0.95

and from work. Average drive time is 32 minutes each way in Westchester County (Westchester County Planning Department, 2003).

Seventy percent attend services once a week or more, and this—along with educational and social activities—represents a major time commitment. The people in the survey are deeply involved in religious communities, yet do not demonstrate the ingroup versus outgroup bias commonly associated with "social identity theory" (Chapter 2).

Table 20 gives the overall statistics on religion (type) and the newspaper use factors (These will explored more in the review of initial hypotheses.) Note that, in descending order, the highest overall mean is for "public affairs" (Factor #3), followed by "entertainment" (Factor #10), "respite" (Factor #5) and "socialization" (Factor #7). Even though Methodists (the majority group) score highest on "Newspaper use: socialization" (Factor #7), across all three groups this factor has the lowest mean score.

Jews have the highest mean on the "public affairs" factor, followed by Methodists and Mormon members. There is no distinction based on minority/majority status.

For the means on "entertainment", Jews and Methodists are closely allied: there is no difference based on majority/minority status.

On the "respite" factor, Jews have the highest mean score, followed again by Methodist and Mormon Church members.

The most important difference is in the means, supporting the initial, launching perspective on the study, is on the "socialization" factor:

Table 21. Factors Ranked in Descending Order of Mean Scores

Rank	Factor Label	N	Mean	SD
1	Religion as spiritual quest	191	4.22	0.74
2	Religion as comfort/security	182	4.14	0.83
3	Ingroup identification: pride and bonding	195	3.81	0.74
4	Ingroup identification: stalwart defender	199	3.70	0.94
5	Religion as time-commitment	192	3.59	0.90
6	Newspaper use: public affairs	193	3.19	0.85
7	Newspaper use: entertainment	197	2.88	0.99
8	Conservatism/fundamentalism	178	2.80	0.94
9	Newspaper use: respite	197	2.50	1.00
10	Ingroup identification: friendship	197	2.39	0.84
11	Political/civic participation	201	2.30	1.04
12	Newspaper use: socialization	196	2.14	0.95

Methodists have the highest means on socialization—using the newspaper as a tool to feel connected to others, since they are apt to feel the most involved in social affairs of the community, as the majority group. They have the closest "fit" with the broader community, since they do not take on the psychological outlook of a minority. However, it is important to realize that "socialization" had the weakest mean score (2.14) and very few respondents view "socialization" as an important use of the newspaper.

5.2.3 Factor Rankings

Based on the factors captioned and analyzed earlier (Chapter 4), descriptive statistics combining results from all three faiths produced the means (shown in Table 21 above) based on a 5–point scale. It is important to examine the results of all three religious groups together to see which factors held the most influence for religious individuals as a whole. It is important to remember that the groups appear relatively similar in their religious behavior and represent a substratum of society that is remarkably religious in a secular world, with 70% attending services one or more times a week. The findings on newspaper use for questor-oriented, religious individuals do not vary that much across religious groups and do not vary significantly at all between the minority groups and the majority Protestant group. Therefore it is important to understand how the factors scored in terms of means, in their entirety.

The one factor in this field of twelve which produced the highest mean score, when combined for the three religious groups, was "Religion as spiritual quest" (4.22 out of 5). Respondents had the highest mean scores on Likert-scale statements which combined to make this composite Factor #8, showing that they take the spiritual quest as very important.

The other pole is represented by "Newspaper Use- Socialization" (2.14 out of 5) which means that respondents' ratings were lowest for the questions which combined as Factor #7, reflecting the use of a newspaper as a link to the social community. Perhaps the religious quest is the center of these individuals' lives and provides them with a self-sufficient community. Since respondents scored the religion as a social time-commitment factor fairly high (3.59), one could presume that the face-to-face socialization that occurs in the house of worship fulfills this need, downplaying the role of the news media as a socialization tool.

5.3 CRITICAL POINTS THAT EMERGED
FROM EXAMINATION OF ORIGINAL HYPOTHESES

In terms of the original hypotheses as a conceptual framework, the following critical results surfaced:

5.3.1 Participation in Political/Civic Affairs by the Majority Group Compared to the Minority

H1a: If individuals belong to the majority, mainstream Protestant group, they will participate more in political/civic affairs.

H1b: If individuals belong to the minority groups, they will participate less in political/civic affairs.

These hypotheses were intended to test whether the majority group (represented by Methodists) participated more in political/civic affairs (Factor #4), compared to the two minority groups, Mormons and Orthodox Jews.

The Jewish group participates the most actively in political/civic affairs (Factor #4), closely followed by Methodists. The largest schism was between these two groups and the Mormons. This indicates rejection of the hypothesis: majority and minority group status was not responsible for the difference in the means.

The greatest difference was between the Mormon group and the other two faiths, with the Mormon mean significantly lower. The Mormon group is a minority in Westchester County, but minority status is not the leading contributor to the difference in the means, since Jews are also a minority.

RESULT: *HYPOTHESES REJECTED*. Membership in majority versus minority groups does not impact political/civic participation.

Table 22. Results of ANOVA Test for Differences in the Mean Between the Three Groups on the Political/Civic Participation Factor (#4)

Faith	N	Means	Std. Dev.
Jewish	68	2.56	1.01
Methodist	68	2.43	1.04
Mormon	65	1.92	0.96

Faith		Mean Difference	Sig.
Jewish	Methodist	.13	.745
	Mormon	.64	.002
Methodist	Jewish	−.13	.745
	Mormon	−.64	.017
Mormon	Jewish	−.64	.002
	Methodist	−.50	.017

	Df	F	Sig.
Between Groups	2	7.357	.001
Within Groups	109		
Total	200		

5.3.2 Use of the Newspaper by the Majority Versus the Minority Group

H2a: If individuals belong to the majority group, they will use the newspaper more for "public affairs"(Factor #3).

H2b: If individuals belong to the minority group, they will use the newspaper less for "public affairs"(Factor #3).

The theory was that the majority group participates more in political/civic affairs, because their religion (type) puts them in the mainstream. The same people who participate heavily both in their church and in the community were thought to be avid newspaper readers (Chapter 1–Table 1). One would think that they need the newspaper to be knowledgeable about public affairs. The overlap between church, community and political life would lead them to read more to be knowledgeable and participate.

The ANOVA test examines the three religions (type), the difference in the mean scores on "newspaper use: public affairs" (Factor #3).

Following the same progression as in Table 22, the Jewish group used the newspaper most for public affairs, followed by the Methodist group, with the greatest distinction with the Mormon group, which tended to participate less in political/civic life and hence read less for public affairs purposes.

The majority/minority distinction did not hold, since Mormons are a minority group, but so are Orthodox Jews, who are a minority even within their own broader Jewish group.

Table 23. Results of ANOVA Test for Differences in the Mean Between the Three Groups on the Newspaper Use—Public Affairs Factor (#3)

Faith	N	Means	Std. Dev.
Jewish	66	3.63	0.72
Methodist	65	3.20	0.77
Mormon	62	2.69	0.78
Total	193	3.19	0.85

Faith		Mean Difference	Sig.
Jewish	Methodist	.44	.005
	Mormon	.94	.000
Methodist	Jewish	−.13	.005
	Mormon	−.13	.001
Mormon	Jewish	−.94	.000
	Methodist	−.51	.001

	Df	F	Sig.
Between Groups	2	24.817	.000
Within Groups	190		
Total	192		

RESULT: *HYPOTHESES REJECTED*. Minority group status was not a determinant of reading the newspaper less for "public affairs."

5.3.3 Service-Attendance and Political Participation

H3a: If individuals attend services more in the majority group they will also participate more in the community.

H3b: If individuals attend services more in the minority groups, they will participate less in the community.

This can be examined through examining the relationship between answers on Question #1, "Attending religious services regularly is important" and the mean on the continuously-scored factor on "political/civic participation" (Factor #4). The majority/minority group distinction does not hold. Methodists and Mormons believe that going to services regularly is important, giving it the highest means, compared to Jews. However, they do not have the highest political/civic participation scores: Jews do. This defeats the hypothesis, which predicted that the minority groups (Jews and Mormons) would shy away from community events as their religious service participation increases, making the house of worship the center of their community lives, since they are minorities and would presumably "fit in" less.

Mormon members attend services the most, but church-going does not lead them to participate more in the general community; in fact, they

Table 24.   Means on Service-Attendance and Political Activity for Each Faith

	Service-Attendance Mean	N	Std. Dev.	Political/Civic Participation	N	Std. Dev.
Jewish	4.24	70	0.82	2.56	68	1.01
Methodist	4.56	70	0.67	2.43	68	1.04
Mormon	4.88	70	0.60	1.92	65	0.96
Composite	4.57	210	0.70	2.31	201	1.04

participate less. This goes against the prevailing literature that individuals who go to services most will also be most active in the community (Chapter 1–Tables 1 and 2). That literature made a presumption that church-going was for social reasons and society was separated into those who were socially involved and those who were not (Lynd, 1929). If these people are attending church for spiritual reasons, it could even lead to a form of withdrawal (Lenski, 1963) and they would be less likely to participate in the broader community.

RESULT: *HYPOTHESES REJECTED.* No relationship exists between church-going among majority group members leading to increased participation in political/civic affairs. Minority group status, coupled with high church-going behavior, does not predict less political/civic participation.

5.3.4 Fundamentalism and Newspaper Subscription.

H4a: If individuals believe more in fundamentalist ideas, they are less likely to read and subscribe to general newspapers.

Individuals who were more fundamentalist and conservative (Factor #12), indeed, were less apt to subscribe to newspapers. This arises from a need to isolate oneself to preserve more conservative values. There is a perception that the media, particularly in the New York area, represent more liberal values.

When subscription and non-subscription issues were examined, non-newspaper subscribers had a higher fundamentalism score. However, using a two-tailed test of significance, with the threshold set at .05, these findings were remarkable but not statistically significant. Non-subscribers had a 2.93

Table 25.   Fundamentalism (Factor #12) and Newspaper Subscription

Newspaper Readership	N	Fundamentalism Mean	Standard Deviation	t-value	df	Sig. (2–tailed)
Non-Subscriber	49	2.92	.84	1.19	173	.24
Subscriber	126	2.73	.98			

composite on questions linked together on the fundamentalist factor-loading, while subscribers to the newspaper had a 2.74 mean on the fundamentalism factor (#12).

RESULT: *HYPOTHESES REJECTED.* Non-subscribers are not shown with any level of statistical significance to be more fundamentalist/conservative than subscribers.

H4b: If individuals believe more in fundamentalist ideas, they are less likely to trust what they read in the newspaper.

The questions on news trust did not hold together (Appendix C-Dropped Questions). The questions initially designed to "tease" out responses on trust were #66, "I trust most of what reporters tell me in secular newspapers"; #67, "News about my religious group is biased in the secular newspaper; #68, "I prefer to read my religious group's own publications for news about my group." These questions did not coalesce into a unified factor.

This points out a shortcoming, only discovered later, in the original research design. Perhaps a coherent picture would emerge by the development of a different instrument specifically devoted to probing trust issues. This would entail a completely different survey.

5.3.5 Social Cohesion and Trust

H5a: If individuals belong to a group whose doctrine stresses social cohesion and ingroup ties, they are less likely to read the general press and more likely to rely on ingroup sources for interpretation of news events.

H5b: If individuals belong to communities with high ingroup ties, they are more apt to turn to clergy for interpretation of news and current events.

These two hypotheses on ingroups' news trust and interpretation of news were built into the original research design, but did not produce any results because the questions on "news trust" did not link together in a significant scale (Appendix C). While three ingroup identification factors did emerge, "news trust" was based on questions #66, #67 and 68 coalescing into a factor and #41, #69, and #70 coalescing into a unified factor. The rotated components matrix loadings showed that this did not result.

When the responses came to be analyzed, the focus of the survey had already shifted from interpretation of news to how the newspaper was used and to religious and ingroup identification in general. Since ingroup ties were minimal to begin with (compared to the need for individual spiritual expression), many of the questions on interpretation of news by community became insignificant, answered in a random manner since respondents tended not to be isolated or overly attached to their communities. Attending church or synagogue was a religious experience sought along with other activities as part of the mix of community life, and closed-in ties were minimal. That is a partial explanation as to why the questions on religious community interpretation of news and ingroup ties did not yield results. In addition, based on observation at services, clergy gave few insights as to news or political events, concentrating more on the inner spiritual experience itself.

RESULT: *Hypotheses cannot be evaluated due to instrumentation.*

5.4 INFORMATION RESULTING FROM THE STUDY: THE QUESTOR MENTALITY AT THE HEART

5.4.1 Questor versus Non-Questor Behavior Overshadows Minority-Majority Distinctions

The study was undertaken to uncover differences between how minority religious group members view the media, particularly the newspaper, compared to majority group members. However, with so many hypotheses denied, it could no longer be posited that there are remarkable differences between how minority religious members, such as Orthodox Jews and Mormons, view the newspaper compared to mainstream Protestants, the largest religious group in the USA population.

That, being said, major distinctions did result from this data and administration of the questionnaire regarding newspaper use and purchase behavior: questors, those individuals who scored high on religion-as-spiritual quest, have very different newspaper perspectives from non-questors, those who scored low on scales of religion-as-spiritual quest. Regardless of denomination, their behavior was remarkably similar.

The results of the study indicate that if questors were grouped together, they would bear more resemblance in behavior (such as heavy service-attendance and media habits) to each other than to fellow faith members who are less preoccupied with the spiritual quest (Chapter 2).

The split in terms of values between questors ("spiritual" individuals) and non-questors ("temporal" individuals), while not stated as such in the hypotheses, emerged through the data analysis in this research investigation as a very powerful polarization.

The questor mentality—almost an ecumenical approach to religion that cuts across individual faiths—emerged as a linchpin to understanding the forces coming to bear on this research in a changed environment. With the mean of all questions dealing with the spiritual quest at 4.22 and the median at 4.0, it is the centripetal focus, the center of gravity for this study.

5.4.2 Questors Use Newspapers and Radio Less than Non-Questors

In newspaper and radio use, frequent users have a lower mean on "religion as spiritual quest" (Factor #8). Those involved in the spiritual quest find it a center of their lives and rely less on newspapers and radio, rich conveyers of information.

The "spiritual quest" is the center of their lives. Examining heavy readers of newspapers, "every day or most days" compared to "occasional to never" readers, a remarkable difference in the means occurs: The mean on questing for regular newspaper readers is 4.14; for non-readers, the mean on questing jumps to 4.42. A regular newspaper reader is less focused on the spiritual quest and more on the practical affairs of everyday life, which newspapers and radio report.

Examining television viewership, there is a difference in the mean between frequent and infrequent viewers, however this difference is not statistically significant.

5.4.3 Questors Read the Business Newspaper Less

At issue is how a questor views the world through the prism of spirituality, how a questor might use media—especially the newspaper—differently from

Table 26. Relationship between Mean Score on the Spiritual Quest (Factor #8) and Media Use

| Newspaper Readership | N | Spiritual Quest (F #8) | | t-value | df | Sig. (2–tailed) |
		Mean	Standard Deviation			
Most days or every day	134	4.13	0.74	2.82	187	.01
Occasionally or never	55	4.35	0.75			

| Radio Listening Weekdays | N | Spiritual Quest (F #8) | | t-value | df | Sig. (2–tailed) |
		Mean	Standard Deviation			
More than 2 hours	46	3.97	.83	3.01	169	.00
Less than 2 hours	125	4.35	.67			

| Television Viewing Weekdays | N | Spiritual Quest (F #8) | | t-value | df | Sig. (2–tailed) |
		Mean	Standard Deviation			
More than 2 hours	67	4.18	.72	0.84	170	.40
Less than 2 hours	105	4.27	.75			

Table 27.   Cross-Tabulation: Service-Attendance and _Wall Street Journal_ Readership

	% Within Attendance at Services		
WSJ Readership	Never to Occasionally (n)	Once a Week (n)	More Than Once a Week (n)
Regular reader	31.3% (15)	23.8% (15)	18.8% (12)
Non-reader	68.8% (33)	76.2% (48)	81.3% (52)
Total	100.0% (48)	100.0% (63)	100.0% (64)

a non-questor. The more information-packed the newspaper (such as _The Wall Street Journal,_ the staple of the business community), the less appeal it would have to someone who defines himself primarily as a spiritual seeker, unless he needs the information for his job. This generalization, by examining the financial newspaper separately, portends the nexus of high questor-lower reader, low questor-higher reader that underlies this research. A key characteristic of heavy questors is attending services at least once, and typically more than once, times a week.

"Regular reader" is defined as someone who reads the Wall Street Journal "every day or most days."

Heavy service-attenders have the least chance of being regular _Wall Street Journal_ readers. Respondents who "never or occasionally" attend religious services are non-readers of the business newspaper, by a 68.8% to 31.3% ratio. Those individuals who go to services once a week are non-readers, by a larger, 76.2% to 23.8% margin. Those who go more than once a week are non-readers, by a 81.3% to 18.8% ratio.

What this means is that if a person rarely attends services, he is less involved in the spiritual life, and there is a 1 in 3 chance that he will read _The Wall Street Journal._ When a person attends services more than once a week, focusing on the spiritual life, there is only a 1 in 5 chance that he will read the business newspaper. Different priorities and uses of time affect the questor versus the non-questor.

5.4.4 Heavy Service-Attenders Read All Newspapers Less

Table 28 illustrates the decline in newspaper readership as service-attendance increases. It is a dramatic progression, although not so sharp a falloff in comparison with the statistics for the information-packed financial publication.

Those individuals who "never or only occasionally" attend services are regular newspaper readers, by a 87.2% to 12.8% margin. When services are attended more than once a week, respondents are readers versus non-readers

Table 28.   Cross-Tabulation: Service-Attendance and Newspaper Reading

	% Within Attendance at Services		
	Never to Occasionally (n)	*Once a Week (n)*	*More Than Once a Week (n)*
Regular newspaper reader	87.2% (41)	80.3% (49)	52.4% (33)
Non-reader	12.8% (6)	19.7% (12)	47.6% (30)
Total	100.0% (47)	100.0% (61)	100.0% (63)

by a 52.4% to 47.6% margin. As an approximation, if a person never or rarely attends services, he is apt to read the newspaper regularly, by a 9:1 margin. Once he spends time attending services more than once a week, the chances of his reading a newspaper regularly are only about 50/50.

Accordingly, it is possible to construct the following profiles, based on high-low services attendance and "questor" versus "non-questor" status.

In the past, it was thought that people who attended church regularly would be more involved in the community and read the newspaper more (Buddenbaum, 1994; Stamm & Weis, 1986). But with people attending church for spiritual, more inward-directed reasons, the converse finding has crystallized. Those preoccupied with matters of faith at an inner level may use their non-work time for spiritual activities and fellowship with others of similar spiritual outlooks.

5.4.5 Mean Scores Differ between Newspaper Readers and Non-Readers on Two out of Three Religiosity Factors

While "Religion as Comfort/Security" (Factor #1) and "religion-as-spiritual quest "(Factor #8)correlate heavily (and inversely) with newspaper reading activity, readership is not affected either way if participation in the house of worship is more for social (Factor #2) than for spiritual reasons. The mean for religion as a time-commitment, as a use of leisure-time socialization, across the three faiths, is 3.60, lower than the 4.45 score for religion as

Table 29.   Polarization of Spiritual and Secular Individuals

Spiritual	*Secular*
High services-attendance pattern	Low services-attendance pattern
High on religion as quest	Low on religion as quest
Very low business newspaper readership	Very high business newspaper readership
Low overall newspaper readership	High overall newspaper readership
Low radio use	Higher radio use

Table 30.   Mean Score of Regular versus Non-Regular Newspaper Readers on the Three Religiosity Factors

	Mean Score on Newspaper Use								
	Read Newspaper Never to Occasionally			Read Newspaper Every day Or Most Days					Sig
Religion Factor	Mean Score	N	Std. Dev.	Mean Score	N	Std. Dev.	t-test	df	(2-tail)
Comfort/Security (Factor #1)	4.35	51	0.59	4.04	128	0.90	2.73	138	.007
Time-Commitment (Factor #2)	3.60	55	0.90	4.13	134	0.75	.058	91	.954
Spiritual quest (Factor #8)	4.45	55	0.67	4.13	134	0.75	2.82	187	.005

a spiritual quest. This indicates that time committed to religion in Westchester County is less for social reasons than for "quest" reasons.

The results of the current study represent a dilution of past findings: those heavily involved in religion as a social time-commitment (Factor #2) did not vary significantly in their newspaper use. In other words, the traditional dichotomy between heavy churchgoers = heavy newspaper users and low churchgoers = low-newspaper users (as reported in the past, when churchgoing was believed to correlate strongly with community social involvement) has weakened.

This change in orientation toward attending church, with the social-time commitment motivation becoming less important (Factor #2) dilutes the traditional notion of heavy churchgoing-heavy socializing-heavy community involvement and newspaper purchase. With house of worship attendance up for spiritual reasons (Stern, 2003:A1), many of the traditionally associated findings—which reflect religion as a social time commitment—are diminishing in importance.

It should be mentioned also that use of the term "religion-as-social" indicator reflects only Factor #2, as defined by the coalescence of statements in this study, and not in any other researcher's work.

Infrequent newspaper readers have a higher mean score on religion as comfort/security (Factor #1) when compared to regular newspaper readers. Although the group that reads the newspaper frequently might have been expected to score high on religion as leisure time-commitment (Factor #2) since they were seen previously as more social, more community-dependent, in this study they did not.

5.5 INGROUP IDENTIFICATION PROVIDES SCANT EVIDENCE OF RELATIONSHIP WITH NEWSPAPER READING

It is remarkable that the three ingroup identification factors have no bearing on newspaper readership, while religiosity, as seen through the prism of spirituality and comfort, has great bearing on newspaper reading habits. The significance figures, based on a two-tailed test are all above the .05 threshold, which signals that is no significance to the difference in the means between regular and infrequent readers of the newspaper in terms of their scores on ingroup identification.

Individual Questions with Highest Means Relate to Religiosity, not Ingroup Identification

Below is a listing in descending hierarchical order of the questions with the highest means in the composite statistics.

Questions (from a total of 81 questions) that emerged as most compelling have to do with serious beliefs about religion and its transmission to the next generation, rather than ingroup identification. It is remarkable, also that none of the highest-scored responses relate to the social experience of religion, more closely allied with the ingroup experience. Rather, they relate to the spiritual quest, existence of God and comfort levels. None relate to ingroup identification, associated with friendship and bonding within the group. The important aspect is the spirituality itself, not the group experience.

Table 31. Comparison of Mean Scores between Regular Readers and Non-Readers on the Three Ingroup Identification Factors

	Mean Score on Newspaper Use								
	Read Newspaper Never to Occasionally			Read Newspaper Every day Or Most Days					
Ingroup Identification Factor	Mean Score	N	Std. Dev.	Mean Score	N	Std. Dev.	t-test	df	Sig
Stalwart defender (Factor #6)	3.72	57	0	3.71	140	0.92	2.34	195	.973
Friendship (Factor #9)	2.33	58	0.78	2.40	138	0.86	−.059	194	.554
Pride and bonding (Factor #11)	3.77	56	0.76	3.83	137	0.73	−5.46	191	.586

Table 32.   Seven Questions/Responses with the Highest Mean Scores

Question	Mean Score	N	Std. Dev.
2. Believe it is important to educate the next generation about my religion	4.68	209	0.65
1. Attending religious services regularly is important	4.56	210	−0.7
3. The religious quest is an important part of my life	4.53	205	0.74
8. Believe in existence of God	4.44	206	1.02
7. Find comfort in my religion during difficult times	4.43	208	0.80
13. The principles of my religious faith serve as guidelines for my actions	4.42	208	0.73
14. My religious faith is a major source of security in my life	4.38	207	0.79

5.5.2 Ingroup Identification Motivation has Consistently Lower Question and Factor Rankings Compared to Religiosity

Both of the highest two factor means relate to religiosity. "Religion as spiritual quest" (4.22) and "religion as comfort" (4.13) rank far higher in the composite statistics than the three ingroup identification factors: "pride and bonding" (3.81); "stalwart defender" (3.69); and a remarkably low mean score (2.39) for "friendship preference," which generally accompanies high ingroup identification.

The primary motivator of individuals attending the services and events is the religious experience itself, rather than ingroup identification: people are attending to express their individual interest and devotion to God, rather than affiliation with a particular group.

To the statement, "I believe all religions are the same" (Q 20), respondents answered with only a 2.61 mean. This suggests that the group that responded to the survey is highly ecumenical in their beliefs. They believe highly in God (4.44 mean on Q 8), attending their own services very faithfully (70% of total respondents attend one or more times a week), yet they believe their counterparts are doing just the same thing they are, expressing their religiosity in their own way.

Chapter Six

Summary

The object of this research at the outset was to solve a problem: Does membership in a minority religious group compared to the majority group lead to different newspaper use behavior?

In order to do this, the author selected two minority groups in the New York area and set out to study the problem through literature research and an empirical survey. The results of the hypothesis-testing showed little distinction between minority and majority group members, in terms of newspaper behavior. However, a careful examination of exploratory findings identified a group of religious people—questors—with remarkable similarity across denominational lines.

Future research could focus on "questors" as a group and determine their newspaper reading traits, demographic and psychographic characteristics, in more detail. What started out as a study of religion (type), ingroup identification and newspaper use emerged as an exploration of religiosity and its effect on newspaper reading behavior.

Scales of religiosity emerged that could be used in future research. The development of the scales is a contribution to the field of communication science.

There were few differences between the faiths individually; religious people of all faiths were remarkably similar in their worldview, when compared to those with less faith. A type of "I'm OK, you're OK" religious relativism surfaced, without any emphasis on the superiority of individual denominations.

This finding is in line with secularization theory which looks at the larger role of religion in society, finding more similarities than differences among faith-based individuals (Froese, 2001; Casanova, 1994). Armfield (2003:9) discusses the pluralism of religious groups and increasingly tolerant attitudes within and among religious groups.

That being said, all of the respondents were moderately religious, averaging about 4.5 out of a 5 on Likert scales of religiosity. They live in an affluent society which is primarily secular, yet are able to maintain spiritual values.

While religious, they are not strong on ingroup identification, averaging around the midpoint or below on most quantitative scales and results showed scant statistical significance. They are attracted to their own type of religion for spiritual reasons but do not disparage other varieties of faith that work for other people. Their religious participation is not for socialization goals but rather for spiritual goals.

Services-going is related inversely to newspaper reading/subscription. Those who go regularly to their house of worship are less apt to spend large amounts of time with the newspaper. Face-contact in the social setting fulfills many of the functions of the media: respite, entertainment, socialization. The need to be informed about the world is not altered by service-attendance and people of high religiosity give more credence to this function of the media.

Constructs about "trust" and the secular newspaper did not hold together under advanced statistical analysis. The statements in the Likert-type scales did not produce any significant "loadings," and this research area had to be abandoned, left to future researchers who could perhaps investigate under a different methodology.

The richest, most important findings came not from the confirmation/rejection of hypotheses, but rather from the analysis of the full set of data. Hence, the book attempts to make its greatest contribution through descriptive insights into religious individuals' lives within secular society, their ingroup identification and newspaper use patterns.

While originally intended as a study of majority versus minority behavior, the distinction between Mormons and Orthodox Jews compared to Methodists, mainstream Protestants, never surfaced, in terms of newspaper behavior. The important information that surfaced about "questors" became of paramount importance, their striking similarities across denominations, rather than their differences.

These are the other most important findings:

- Service-attendance and political/civic participation did not co-vary along the traditional lines of greater service activity—greater community involvement, since the service-attendance was primarily for spiritual reasons, more associated with withdrawal and inner activity than for social reasons;
- Newspaper readership declines with increased service-attendance;
- For the business newspaper *(The Wall Street Journal)* this trend is more pronounced: by an even greater margin, heavy service attenders are non-readers of the financial publication;

- A polarization exists between spiritual seekers (questors, those involved heavily in their house of worship) and temporal individuals (non-questors, who shy away from religious involvement) in terms of newspaper and radio use.

CONCLUDING REMARKS

The author herself changed a great deal through the journey and visitation of the various houses of worship. Places that seemed foreign became familiar; those that were familiar became foreign as she spoke to congregants and realized that their experiences were not what she anticipated.

The most interesting aspect of suburbia today is the complete homogenization. With similar malls, televisions in every bank lobby, no group is that separate. Perhaps some of the findings would have held—about insularity— had the research occurred among the Amish, Mennonites, or the Amana colonies in Iowa.

In contemporary suburbia, no group is that disparate, reflecting John Dunne's noteworthy phrase that "no man is an island" (Meditation 23). Mass media is ubiquitous. You are exposed to television in the lobby of a building no matter how adverse you are to mass media penetration.

So, it becomes a matter of degrees. Those who choose to make the church or temple their second home, their natural habitat, are embracing a more detached view of society—and this is reflected in their media choice. The idea of a religious minority pursuing a detached lifestyle is far from the way we live in suburban America. Religiosity is a matter of degree, and that can affect how we view media.

The extent to which spirituality is expressed and comes to the surface determines how we relate to institutions such as media, not the brand of "religion" or its particular manifestation.

The relationship between religion and media can not be described as a dialectic but as a series of overlapping conversations. While those attempting to assert religious control may urge adherents to shun media, they are often the subjects of controversial reportage. Hence, their attempts to disassociate from media ultimately fail, in that prepared statements to counteract what they perceive as media propaganda become necessary and the center cannot hold. It is impossible in today's world for even the most devout, most separatist groups, to carve out a world beyond the realm of secular media. Hence, the veil that divides the ascetic from the most worldly person is rather thin and the separation is less than complete. Still, it is a force that exists and must be reckoned with by scholars of both religion and communications studies.

Appendices

APPENDIX A: SURVEY

To what extent you agree or disagree with the following:

Question Number and Content	Disagree strongly		Neutral	Agree strongly	
1 Attending religious services regularly is important.	1	2	3	4	5
2 I believe it is important to educate the next generation about my religion.	1	2	3	4	5
3 The religious quest is an essential part of my life.	1	2	3	4	5
4 Attending religious services gives me the opportunity to make new friends.	1	2	3	4	5
5 I believe the best friends are those that share your religion.	1	2	3	4	5
6 My whole approach to life is based on my religion.	1	2	3	4	5
7 I find comfort in my religion during difficult times.	1	2	3	4	5
8 I doubt the existence of God.	1	2	3	4	5
9 I care what members of my religious community think of me.	1	2	3	4	5
10 I identify with my religious community more than the general society around me.	1	2	3	4	5
11 I feel proud when a member of my congregation excels or does something good.	1	2	3	4	5
12 I am more loyal to my religious group than to any other societal group.	1	2	3	4	5
13 The principles of my religious faith serve as guidelines for my actions.	1	2	3	4	5
14 My religious faith is a major source of security in my life.	1	2	3	4	5

(continued)

Question Number and Content	Disagree strongly		Neutral	Agree strongly	
15 I am against children from my faith marrying persons not in my religion.	1	2	3	4	5
16 Children of my faith should also participate in other youth activities in the community.	1	2	3	4	5
17 I am willing to take action if the interests of my religious group are threatened.	1	2	3	4	5
18 During my free time I am mostly involved with activities of my religious group.	1	2	3	4	5
19 I have many friends belonging to religions different from my own.	1	2	3	4	5
20 I believe that all religions are more or less the same.	1	2	3	4	5
21 Being a member of a church or synagogue is just a a social custom for me.	1	2	3	4	5
22 Members of my congregation have helped me through difficult times.	1	2	3	4	5

How frequently do you engage in each of the following behaviors?

Question Number and Content	Almost Never	Seldom	Occasionally	Very Often	Often
23 Pray privately or meditate	1	2	3	4	5
24 Attend religious education activities	1	2	3	4	5
25 Attend social activities from my congregation	1	2	3	4	5
26 Contribute financially to my house of worship beyond required dues (tithes) (pledges)	1	2	3	4	5
27 Read magazines and religious publications from my group	1	2	3	4	5
28 Read Biblical teachings and scriptures on my own	1	2	3	4	5
29 Cooperate with most decisions made by leaders at my house of worship	1	2	3	4	5
30 Interact with others outside my faith	1	2	3	4	5
31 Vote in elections	1	2	3	4	5
32 Go to meetings about civic issues	1	2	3	4	5
33 Contribute money or time to political parties	1	2	3	4	5
34 Participate in environmental cleanups	1	2	3	4	5
35 Attend secular cultural events	1	2	3	4	5
36 Attend political events	1	2	3	4	5
37 Use the public library	1	2	3	4	5
38 Read a newspaper from my local community or metropolitan area	1	2	3	4	5

To what extent do you agree or disagree with the following?

Question Number and Content	Disagree strongly		Neutral	Agree strongly	
39 Missing the daily newspaper makes me feel disconnected from the outside world.	1	2	3	4	5
40 Reading the newspaper every morning is part of my routine.	1	2	3	4	5
41 If what I read in the newspaper is discordant with teaching of my religion I read it anyway.	1	2	3	4	5
42 I read most of my news in text format, either in the newspaper or on the Internet.	1	2	3	4	5
43 I get most of my news from radio or TV.	1	2	3	4	5
44 I'm not oriented toward news and pay almost no attention to it.	1	2	3	4	5
45 I discuss the news with friends in my religious group.	1	2	3	4	5
46 I have my favorite newspaper columnists.	1	2	3	4	5

Media Usage Patterns

How often do you read a newspaper?

(Check One) Every day _____
Most days _____
Only on weekends _____
Occasionally _____
Never _____

How do you get your newspaper? (Check one)

Paid subscription to home ____
Paid subscription at work ____
Off the newsstand _____
Do not buy a newspaper _____
Other _____

How many hours per day do you watch television?
Weekdays (Monday–Friday) _____
Weekends(Saturday–Sunday) _____

How many hours per day do you listen to radio?
Weekdays (Monday–Friday) _____
Weekends (Saturday–Sunday) _____

Which secular newspapers do you read? (Check as many as apply)
The New York Times _____
The Wall Street Journal _____
The Journal News _____

How often do you engage in each of these behaviors?

Question Number and Content	Almost Never		About ½ the time		Almost Always
47 Find out about what is at the movies by reading the newspaper.	1	2	3	4	5
48 Find out what is on television by reading the newspaper.	1	2	3	4	5
49 Find out about sales in stores in the newspaper.	1	2	3	4	5
50 Find out about stocks or business concerns in the newspaper.	1	2	3	4	5
51 Plan vacations using the newspaper. 1	2	3	4	5	
52 Read the editorial pages of the newspaper.	1	2	3	4	5
53 Read the newspaper to be informed about political issues.	1	2	3	4	5
54 Read the newspaper to be a lively conversationalist	1	2	3	4	5
55 Read the newspaper primarily to see if friends or relatives are mentioned. 1	2	3	4	5	
56 Put talking to friends above what is going on in the community above reading facts from the newspaper	1	2	3	4	5

To what extent do you agree or disagree with the following statements:

Question Number and Content	Disagree strongly		Neutral	Agree strongly	
57 I seem more well informed to others when I have read the newspaper.	1	2	3	4	5
58 I relax when I read the newspaper.	1	2	3	4	5
59 I escape from personal problems when I read the newspaper.	1	2	3	4	5
60 I escape from livelihood concerns when I read the newspaper.	1	2	3	4	5
61 I take my mind off other things when I read the newspaper.	1	2	3	4	5
62 I consider newspaper columnists almost like personal friends.	1	2	3	4	5
63 I follow the lives of celebrities in the newspaper.	1	2	3	4	5
64 I feel connected to important people through the newspaper.	1	2	3	4	5
65 I read gossip/advice columns in the newspaper.	1	2	3	4	5
66 I trust most of what reporters tell me in secular newspapers.	1	2	3	4	5
67 News about my religious group is biased in the secular newspaper.	1	2	3	4	5
68 I prefer to read my religious group's own publications for news about my group.	1	2	3	4	5

69	I trust my clergyman's analysis of local news events more than what is reported in secular newspapers.	1 2	3	4 5	
70	I trust my clergyman's analysis of world/national news events more than what is reported in secular newspapers.	1 2	3	4 5	
71	My main source of news is friends in my religious community.	1 2	3	4 5	
72	My most trustworthy source of news is friends in my religious community.	1 2	3	4 5	
73	I tend to be conservative on most issues.	1 2	3	4 5	
74	I think abortion should be outlawed.	1 2	3	4 5	
75	My political beliefs vary from liberal to conservative based on the subject under discussion.	1 2	3	4 5	
76	Government has grown too big.	1 2	3	4 5	
77	Politics is important to me.	1 2	3	4 5	
78	Every word of the Bible is true.	1 2	3	4 5	
79	The USA is under God's protection.	1 2	3	4 5	
80	Public officials should embody their religion's ethics.	1 2	3	4 5	
81	The president's authority is derived from God.	1 2	3	4 5	

Demographic Information

Age _____

Highest school or college year completed (check one)

Did not graduate high school _____

High school graduation _____

Some college _____

College graduate _____

Master's degree _____

Doctoral degree _____

(Check one) Male _____   Female _____

Occupation: _____

Household income Under $50,000 _____

$ 50,001–$ 75,000 _____

$ 75,001–$100,000 _____

$100,001–$150,000 _____

$150,001–$200,000 _____

$ over $200,000 _____

Religious Denomination (check one)

Member of this congregation _____

Visitor to this congregation _____

Name of other congregation if you are visiting
here but hold a membership elsewhere _____

How often do you attend religious services?
  (Check one)Four or more times each week _____
    One to three times each week _____
    Once a week _____
    One to three times a month _____
    Six to eleven times a year _____
    One to five times a year _____
    Never _____

Marital Status:
(Check one) Single _____   Married _____
                          Living with Partner
Other: _____
Number of children under age 18 living at home _____

APPENDIX B: ORIGINAL CONSTRUCTS

Religiosity—General Attitude Scale

1. Attending religious services regularly is important.
2. I believe it is important to educate the next generation about my religion.
6. My whole approach to life is based on my religion.
13. The principles of my religious faith serve as guidelines for my actions.

Religiosity—Questor Orientation

7. The religious quest is an essential part of my life.
8. I doubt the existence of God.
28. Read Biblical teachings and scriptures on my own

Religiosity—Social Orientation

4. Attending religious services gives me the opportunity to make new friends.
18. During my free time I am mostly involved with activities of my religious group
20. I believe that all religions are more or less the same
21. Being a member of a church or synagogue is just a social custom for me

Religiosity—Security/Comfort Orientation

7. I find comfort in my religion during difficult times.
14. My religious faith is a major source of security in my life.
22. Members of my congregation have helped me through difficult times

Religiosity—Behavior

23. Pray privately or meditate
24. Attend religious education activities
25. Attend social activities from my congregation
26. Contribute financially to my house of worship beyond required dues
27. Read magazines and religious publications from my group
29. Cooperate with most decisions made by leaders at my house of worship

Ingroup Identification

7. I believe that the best friends are those that share your religion.
9. I care what members of my religious community think of me.
10. I identify with my religious community more than the general society around me
11. I feel proud when a member of my congregation excels or does something good
12. I am more loyal to my religious group than to any other societal group.
15. I am against children from my faith marrying persons not in my religion.
16. Children of my faith should also participate in other youth activities in the community.
17. I am willing to take action if the interests of my religious group are threatened
19. I have many friends belonging to religions different from my own
30. Interact with others outside my faith

Civic Participation/Community Integration

31. Vote in elections
32. Go to meetings about civic issues
33. Contribute money or time to political parties
34. Participate in environmental cleanups

35. Attend secular cultural activities
36. Attend political events
37. Use the public library
38. Read a newspaper from my local community or metropolitan area
77. Politics is important to me

Newspaper Reading Habits

40. Reading the newspaper every morning is part of my routine,
39. Missing the daily newspaper makes me feel disconnected from the outside world
42. I read most of my news in text format, either in the newspaper or on the Internet
43. I get most of my news from radio or TV
44. I'm not oriented toward news and pay almost no attention to it

Clergy/Religious Influence on News Habits/Interpretation

41. If what I read in the newspaper is discordant with teachings of my religion, I read it anyway
69. I trust my clergyman's analysis of local new events more than what is reported in secular newspapers
70. I trust my clergyman's analysis of world/national news events more than what is reported in secular newspapers.

Religious Friends' Influence on News Habits/ Interpretation

45. I discuss the news with friends in my religious group
56. Put talking to friends about what is going on in the community above reading facts from the newspaper
71. My main source of news is friends in my religious community
72. My most trustworthy source of news s friends in my religious community

Uses—Entertainment

47. Find out about what is at the movies by reading the newspaper.
48. Find out what is on television by reading the newspaper
51. Plan vacations using the newspaper.

Uses—Information

49. Find out about sales in stores in the newspaper.
50. Find out about stocks or business concerns in the newspaper
57. I seem more well informed to others when I have read the newspaper.

Uses—Public Affairs

52. Read the editorial page of the newspaper
53. Read the newspaper to be informed about political issues.
54. Read the newspaper to be a lively conversationalist

Uses—Social

55. Read the newspaper primarily to see if friends or relatives are mentioned.
62. I consider newspaper columnists almost like personal friends
63. I follow the lives of celebrities in the newspaper.
64. I feel connected to important people through the newspaper.
65. I read gossip/advice columns in the newspaper.
46. I have my favorite newspaper columnists

Uses—Respite

58. I relax when I read the newspaper.
59. I escape from personal problems when I read the newspaper.
60. I escape from livelihood concerns when I read the newspaper.
61. I take my mind off other things when I read the newspaper.

Trust-Secular Papers

66. I trust most of what reporters tell me in secular newspapers
67. News about my religious group is biased in the secular newspaper
68. I prefer to read my religious group's own publications for news about my group

Conservatism

73. I tend to be conservative on most issues
74. I think abortion should be outlawed
75. My political beliefs vary from liberal to conservative based on the subject under discussion
76. Government has grown too big.

Fundamentalism

78. Every word of the Bible is true
79. The USA is under God's protection
80. Public officials should embody their religion's ethics
81. The President's authority is derived from God

APPENDIX C: QUESTIONS THAT DID NOT "LOAD" INTO FACTORS FROM THE CATEGORIZATION OF "DROPPED QUESTIONS"

Religiosity

4. Attending religious services gives me the opportunity to make new friends.

Ingroup Identification

16. Children of my faith should also participate in other youth activities of the community.

Civic Participation

31. Vote in elections
34. Participate in environmental cleanups
35. Attend secular cultural activities
37. Use the public library
77. Politics is important to me

News Habits

43. I get most of my news from radio or TV.
44. I'm not oriented toward news and pay almost no attention to it.

Clergy

69. I trust my clergyman's analysis of local news events more than what is reported in secular newspapers.
70. I trust clergyman's analysis of world/national news events more than what is reported in secular newspapers.

Religious Friends

45. I discuss the news with friends in my religious group.
72. My most trustworthy source of news is friends in my religious community.
71. My main source of news is friends in my religious community.

Public Affairs

53. Read the newspaper to be informed about political issues
54. Read a newspaper to be a lively conversationalist
55. Read the newspaper primarily to see if friends or relatives are mentioned
57. I seem more well informed to others when I have read the newspaper.
58. I relax when I read the newspaper.
62. I consider newspaper columnists almost like personal friends.

Trusting Reporters

66. I trust most of what reporters tell me in secular newspapers.
67. News about my religious group is biased in the secular newspaper.
68. I prefer to read my religious group's own publications for news about my group.

Conservative Ideology

73. I tend to be conservative on most issues.
75. My political beliefs vary from liberal to conservative based on the subject under discussion.
76. Government has grown too big.

APPENDIX D: WRITE-IN COMMENTS

These were write-in comments in response to Likert-scale questions on the survey:

Q4. Attending religious services gives me the opportunity to make new friends . . .

"and to Love God"

Q22. Members of my congregation have helped me through difficult times . . . "

through (the) Prayer chain"

Q56. I relax when I read the newspaper . . .

"Not in these times"

Q74. I think abortion should be outlawed
      "under special conditions"
      "not outlawed but restricted" (2)
Q78. Every word of the Bible is true . . .
      "The essence is true."
      "as long as it has been translated correctly"
Q79. The USA is under God's protection.
      "Conditionally, depending on whether we obey His commandments"
      "I hope so."
      "All the world is"
      "The whole world is important to God"
Q81. The President's authority is derived from God
      "Indirectly. The Constitution is inspired by God."
      "Depends on who the President is!"
Q56. In response to several questions regarding talking to friends about the
      news . . .
      "I develop an opinion based on talking to friends rather than interpret-
      ing or reading facts in the newspaper."

Bibliography

Abrams, D. & Hogg, M., eds. 1990. *Social Identity Theory: Constructive and Critical Advances*. London: Harvester Wheatsheaf.

Althaus, S. L. & Tewksbury, D. 2000. Patterns of Internet and Traditional News Media Use in a Networked Community. *Political Communications*, 17 (Jan), 21–46.

American Jewish Congress. Research Department. Phone interview. 4/12/2003.

Ang, I. 1991. *Desperately Seeking the Audience*. London: Routledge.

Armfield, G. G. 2003. A Structural Equation Model of Religiosities Effect on Mass Media Use and Civic Participation. Paper before Association of Educators in Journalism and Mass Communication, Kansas City, Mo.

Armstrong, K. 1993. *A History of God*. New York: Ballantine Books.

Baltus, R. K. 1988. *Personal Psychology for Life and Work*. New York: Gregg Division.

Barwise, T. P & Ehrenberg, A. S. C. 1988. *Television and its audience*. London: Sage.

Basu, S. 1999. Comprehending the Psychology of Intergroup Relations: Prospects for the Reduction of Prejudice. Cambridge, MA: Massachusetts Institute of Technology Working Papers.

Berger, P. L. 1966. *The Social Construction of Reality, A Treatise in the Sociology of Knowledge*. Garden City, NY: Doubleday.

Berelson, B. 1949. What Missing the Newspaper Means? in P. Lazarsfeld & F. Stanton, eds., *Communication Research*, 1948–49. New York: Harper & Row.

Billig, M. 2002. Henri Tajfel's 'Cognitive aspects of prejudice' and the psychology of bigotry. *British Journal of Social Psychology*, 41(2) June, 171–189.

Blumler, J. G. & Katz, E. 1974. *The Uses of Mass Communication*. Newbury Park, CA: Sage.

Bogart, L. 1996. Research as an instrument of power, in E Dennis & E Wartella, eds. *American communication research: The remembered history*, 135–146. Mahwah, NJ: Erlbaum.

Bornman, E. & Mynhardt, J. C. 1991. Social identity and intergroup contact in South Africa with specific reference to the work situation. *Genetic, Social and General Psychology Monographs*, 117 (4), 439–463.

113

Branscombe, N. R. & Wann, D. L. 1994. Collective self-esteem consequences of out-group derogation when a valued social identity is on trial. *European Journal of Social Psychology*, 24, 641–657.

Brewer, M. B. & Miller, N. 1984. Beyond the contact hypothesis: Theoretical perspectives on desegregation, in N. Miller & M. B. Brewer, eds. *Groups in contact: The psychology of desegregation,* 281–302. Orlando, FL: Academic Press.

Brewer, M. B. and Miller, N. 1979. Ingroup bias in the minimal intergroup situation: A cognitive motivational analysis. *Psychological Bulletin*, 86, 307–324.

Brewer, M. B. & Gardner, W. 1996. Who is this 'we'? Levels of collective identity and self representations. *Journal of Personality & Social Psychology,* 71 (1) July, 83–93.

Brown, R. 1998. Intergroup Relations: A Field with a Short History but a Long Future, in J. Adair, D. Belanger & K. Dion, eds. *Advances in Psychological Science,* Vol. 1: *Social, Personal, and Cultural Aspects,* 73–91. East Sussex, UK: Psychology Press Ltd.

Buddenbaum, J. M. 1986. An analysis of religion news coverage in three major newspapers. *Journalism Quarterly*, 63, 600–606.

Buddenbaum, J. M. 1992. Agenda-Setting by Religious Organizations in the 1992 Presidential Election Campaign: A Study of Six Middletown Congregations. Paper before the Midwest Association for Public Opinion Research Annual Meeting, Chicago, Illinois, November 14.

Buddenbaum, J. M. 1993. Religion, Politics, and Media Use: A Study of Six Middletown Congregations during the 1992 Presidential Campaign, Working Paper.

Buddenbaum, J. M. 1993a. The Economy as a Religious Issue. Paper before the Society for the Scientific Study of Religion Annual Meeting, Raleigh, North Carolina, October 29–31.

Buddenbaum, J. M. 1994. Characteristics of Readers of Religious Publications for Political Information. Paper before the Association for Education in Journalism and Mass Communication, National Convention, Atlanta, Georgia, August.

Buddenbaum, J. M. 1996. The Role of Religion in Newspaper Trust, Subscribing and Use for Political Information, in D. Stout and J. Buddenbaum, eds, *Religion and Mass Media: Audiences and Adaptations.* Thousand Oaks, CA: Sage.

Buddenbaum, J. M. 1999. Unpublished Paper. Association for Education in Journalism and Mass Communication. New Orleans, La., August.

Buddenbaum, J. M. 2001. Christian Perspectives on Mass Media, in D. Stout and J Buddenbaum, eds. *Religion and Popular Culture: Studies on the Interaction of Worldviews.* Ames: Iowa State University Press.

Bulman, R. F. 1991. Myth of Origin: Civil Religion and Presidential Politics. *Journal of Church and State*, Summer, 525–539.

Capozza, D. & Brown, R., eds. 2000. *Social identity processes: trends in theory and research.* London: Sage Publications.

Casanova, J. 1994. *Public Religions in the Modern World.* Chicago, IL: University of Chicago Press.

Cassata, M. & Asante, M K. 1979. *Mass Communication: Principles and Practices.* New York: Macmillan.

Cohen, N. J. 1990. *The Fundamentalist Phenomenon.* Grand Rapids, MI: Eerdmans Publishing Company.

Collins, C. 1997. Viewer letters as audience research: The case of Murphy Brown. *Journal of Broadcasting & Electronic Media*, Winter, 41(1), 109–132.

Davis, R. & Owen, D. 1998. *New media and American politics.* New York: Oxford University Press.

DeFleur, M. 1970. *Theories of Mass Communication Research.* New York: McKay.

DeFleur, M & Ball-Rokeach, S. 1989. *Theories of Mass Communication*, 5th ed. White Plains, N.Y.: Longman.

DeLubicz, R. A. S. 1978. *Symbol and the Symbolic.* Brookline, MA: Autumn Press.

Diehl, M. 1990. The minimal group paradigm: Theoretical explanations and empirical findings, in W Stroebe and M Hewstone, eds., *European Review of Social Psychology*, Vol. 1, 263–292. Chichester, UK: Wiley.

Dillon, M. & Goldstein, M. 1984. *Multivariate Analysis: Methods and Applications.* New York: John Wiley & Sons.

Dollar, G. W. 1973. *A History of Fundamentalism in America.* Greenville, SC: Bob Jones University Press.

Dominick, J. R. 1990. *The Dynamics of Mass Communication*, 4th edition. New York: McGraw-Hill.

Doosje, B., Spears, R., & Ellemers, N. 2002. Social Identity as both cause and effect: the development of group identification in response to anticipated and actual changes in the intergroup status hierarchy. *British Journal of Social Psychology*, 41 (1) Mar, 57–77.

Eighmey, J. & McCord, L. 1998. Adding value in the information age: Uses and gratifications of sites on the World Wide Web. *Journal of Business Research*, 41, 187–194.

Festinger, L. A. 1957. *A Theory of Cognitive Dissonance.* New York: Harper & Row.

Finnegan, F. R., Jr. & Viswanath, K. 1988. Community ties and the use of cable TV and newspapers in a Midwest suburb. *Journalism Quarterly*, 65, 563–473.

Fletcher, G. O., & Fitness, J. 1996. *Knowledge structures in close relationships: A social psychological approach.* Mahwah, NJ: Lawrence Erlbaum.

Froese, P. 2001. Hungary for Religion: A Supply-Side Interpretation of the Hungarian Religious Revival. *Journal for the Scientific Study of Religion*, 40 (2), 251–269.

Funk & Wagnall's *New International Dictionary of the English Language.* 1987. New York:

Galanter, M. 1989. *Cults, Faith, Healing and Coercion.* New York: Oxford University Press.

Gans, H. J. 1962. *The Urban Villagers: Group and Class in the Life of Italian-Americans.* NY: Free Press of Glencoe.

Gardner, W. L., Brewer, M. B., and Pickett, C. L. 2000. Social Exclusion and Selective Memory: How the Need to Belong Influences Memory for Social Events. *Personality and Social Psychology Bulletin*, 26 Apr, 486–96.

Granovetter, M. 1978. Threshold models for collective Behavior, *American Journal of Sociology*, 83, 1420–1443.

Grossberg, L., Wartella, E. & Whitney, D. 1998. *Mediamaking: mass media in popular culture.* California: Sage.

Harstone, M. & Augoustinos, M. 1995. The minimal group paradigm: categorization into two versus three groups. *European Journal of Social Psychology,* 25, 179–193.

Hart, S. 1992. The rationality of culture and the culture of rationality: Some Husserlian proposals. *Philosophy East & West,* 42(4), Oct, 643–661.

Hedstrom, Stu. The spectacle of Superbowl XXXVII [O}. http:/journalism.smcvt.edu/echo/1.29.03/sports.htmAccessed on 11/20/03.

Heilman, S. C. and Cohen, S. M. 1989. *Cosmopolitans and Parochials: Modern Orthodox Jews in America.* Chicago and London: University of Chicago Press.

Heikkinen, K. J, & Reese, S. 1986. Newspaper readers and a new information medium: Information need and channel orientation as predictors of videotext adoption. *Communication Research,* 13, 19–36.

Herberg, W. 1955. *Protestant, Catholic, Jew: An Essay in American Religious Sociology.* Garden City, NY: Doubleday.

Hoover, S. M. & Clark, L. S. 2002. *Practicing Religion in the Age of Media.* NY: Columbia University Press.

Hornsey, M. & Hogg, M. 2002. The effects of status on subgroup relations. *British Journal of Social Psychology,* 41(2) June, 203–219.

Janowitz, M. 1952. *The Community Press in an Urban Setting.* Glencoe, IL: Free Press.

Jorstad, E. 1986. *Being Religious in America.* Minneapolis: Augsburg Press.

Kanter, R. M. 1972. *Commitment and Continuity.* Cambridge, MA: Harvard University Press.

Katz, E., Blumler, J. G. and Gurevitch, M. 1974. Uses and Gratifications Research, in *The Uses of Mass Communications,* J. G. Blumler and E. Katz, eds. Beverly Hills, CA: Sage Publications.

Katz, E., Gurevitch, M. & Haas, H. 1973. On the Use of Mass Media for Important Things. *American Sociological Review,* 38 Apr, 164–181.

Kerlinger, F. N. 1986. *Foundations of Behavioral Research,* 3rd Edition. London: Holt, Rinehart & Winston.

Kidder, L. H. & Stewart, V. M. 1975. *The Psychology of Intergroup Relations: Conflict and Consciousness.* New York: McGraw-Hill.

Korgaonkar, P. 1999. A multivariate analysis of Web usage. *Journal of Advertising Research,* 39 (2) Mar/Apr, 53–68.

Kosmin, B. 2002. As secular as they come. *Moment.* June. 44–49.

Kraut, R. E. & Attewell, P. 1997. Media use in a global corporation: Electronic mail and organizational knowledge, in S. Kiesler, Ed., *Culture of the internet,* 323–342. Mahwah, NJ: Erlbaum.

Kreps, G. 1990. *Organizational Communications.* White Plains, NY: Longman Press.

Lasswell, H. D. 1948. The Structure and Function of Communication in Society, in *The Communication of Ideas,* L. Bryson, ed. New York: Harper & Brothers.

Lazarsfeld, P., Berelson, B. & Gaudet, J. 1944. *The People's Choice.* New York: Duell, Sloan, and Pearce.

Leathers, G. 1986. *Successful Nonverbal Communication Principles and Application.* NY: Macmillan Publishing Company.

Lenski, G. 1963. *The Religious Factor: A Sociological Study of Religion's Impact on Politics, Economics, and Family Life.* Garden City, NY: Doubleday.

Levy, M. R. & Windahl, S. 1985. The concept of audience activity, in K. E. Rosengreen, L. A. Wenner, and R. Palmgreen, eds., *Media Gratifications Research; Current Perspectives,* 109–122. Beverly Hills: Sage.

Lin, C. A. 1999. Online-service adoption likelihood. *Journal of Advertising Research,* 39 (2), 79–89.

Lin, C. A. 1993. Modeling the gratification-seeking process of television viewing. *Human Communication Research,* 20, 224–244.

Lynd, R. S. & H. M. 1929. *Middletown: A Study in American Culture.* Muncie, IL: Ball State University Press.

Maslow, A. 1954. *Motivation and Personality.* New York: Harper & Row.

Maslow, A. 1982. *Toward a Psychology of Being,* 2nd edition. New York: Van Nostrand Reinhold.

McQuail, D. 1994. *Mass communication theory: An introduction,* 3rd edition. Thousand Oaks, CA: Sage.

McQuail, D. 1987. *Mass Communication Theory: An Introduction,* 2nd edition. London: Sage.

Merton, R. K. 1950. *Continuities in Social Research.* Glencoe, IL: Free Press.

Morley, D. 1992. *Television, Audiences and Cultural Studies.* London: Routledge.

Newhagen, J. E. & Rafaeli, S. 1996. Why communication researchers should study the Internet: A dialogue. *Journal of Communication,* 461, 4–13.

Ostling, R. N. & J. K. 1999. *Mormon America: The Power and the Promise.* San Francisco: Harper.

Palmgreen, P., Wenner, L. A. & Rosengren, K .E. 1985. Uses and Gratifications Research, The Past Ten Years, in *Media Gratifications Research: Current Perspectives.* Beverly Hills, CA: Sage.

Perse, E. M. & Dunn, D.. G. 1998. The Utility of Home Computers and Media Use: Implications of Multimedia and Connectivity. *Journal of Broadcasting and Electronic Media.* 42:2 (Fall), 435–456.

Puddifoot, J. E. 1997. Psychological reaction to perceived erasure of community boundaries. *Journal of Social Psychology,* 137 (3), June, 343–356.

Rafaeli, S. 1986. The Electronic Bulletin Board. *Computers and the Social Sciences,* 2, 123–136.

Reimer, B. 1998. Crisis? What crisis? Analysing audience studies. *Nordicom Review* 19,1135–1142.

Reina, L. 1995. Who's Reading Newspapers? *Editor & Publisher,* 128 (45), 24–26.

Rogers, E. M. 1983. *Diffusion of Innovations.* New York: Free Press.

Rosenthal, D. A. & Hrynevich, C. 1985. Ethnicity and ethnic identity: a comparative study of Greek-, Italian- and Anglo-Australian adolescents. *International Journal of Psychology,* 20, 723–742.

Rubin, A. M. 1984. An Examination of Television Viewing Motives. *Journal of Communication Research,* 8:3, 14165.

Rushkoff, D. 2003. *Nothing Sacred: The Truth about Judaism.* New York: Crown Publishers.

Seiter, E., Borchers H, Kreutzner, G. & Eva-Maria W., eds. 1989. *Remote Control: Television, Audiences and Cultural Power.* London: Routledge.

Sherif & Sherif, M. 1953. *Groups in harmony and tension: An integration of studies on intergroup relations*. New York: Harper & Brothers.

Sherry, J. L. 2001. Toward an etiology of media use motivations: The role of temperament in media use. *Communication Monographs*. 68, 274–88.

Simmel, G. 1955. *Conflict*. New York: Free Press.

Simpson, G. E. & Yinger, M. J. 1985. *Racial and Cultural Minorities: An Analysis of Prejudice and Discrimination*. New York: Plenum Press.

Southwick, J. H. Acting Director of Research, Research Office, General Board of Global Ministries, United Methodist Church Central Office. Phone interview. 3/12/2003.

Stamm, K. & Weis, R. 1986. The Newspaper and Community Integration: A Study of Ties to a Local Church Community. *Communication Research*, 13: 125–137.

Stark, R. & Bainbridge, W. S. 1985. *The Future of Religion*. Berkeley, CA: University of California Press.

Stern, G. 2003. Mainline Protestant Flock Thins: Change leaving churches behind, *The Journal News*, May 4, 2003, A1.

Stern, G. 2003a. Phone interview, 4/03/2003.

Stout, D. 1996. Protecting the Family: Mormon Teachings about Mass Media, in D. Stout and J Buddenbaum, eds, *Religion and Mass Media: Audiences and Adaptations*. Thousand Oaks, CA: Sage.

Stout, D., Scott, D. & Dennis M. 1996. Mormons, Mass Media and the Interpretive Audience, in D. Stout & J Buddenbaum, eds, *Religion and Mass Media. Audiences and Adaptations*. Thousand Oaks, CA: Sage.

Stout, D. & Buddenbaum, J., eds. 1996. *Religion and Mass Media: Audiences and Adaptations*. Thousand Oaks, CA: Sage.

Stout, D. & Buddenbaum, J., eds. 2001. *Religion and Popular Culture: Studies on the Interaction of Worldviews*. Ames: Iowa State University Press.

Suzuki, S. 1998. Ingroup and outgroup communication patterns. *Communication Research*, 25(2), Apr, 154–83.

Swatos, W. H., Jr., & Christiano, K. J. 2000. Secularization theory: The course of a concept, *in* W. H. Swatos, Jr. and D. V. A Olsen, eds., *The secularization debate*, 1–20. Lanham: Rowman & Littlefield.

Tajfel, H. 1978. *The Social Psychology of Minorities*. Minority Rights Group.

Tajfel, H. 1981. *Human Groups and Social Categories*. Cambridge, UK: Cambridge University Press.

Tajfel, H. & Turner, J. C. 1986. The Social Identity Theory of Intergroup Behavior, 7–24, in S. Worchel & W. G. Austin, eds., *Psychology of Intergroup Relations*. Chicago: NelsonHall.

Taylor, D. M. & McKirnan, D. J. 1984. A five-stage model of intergroup relations. *British Journal of Social Psychology*, 23, 291–300.

Turkle, S. 1996. Parallel lives: Working on identity in virtual space, in D. Grodin & T. R. Lindlof, eds., Constructing the self in a mediated world: Inquiries in social construction, 156–175. Thousand Oaks, CA: Sage.

Turner, J. C. 1981. The Experimental social psychology of intergroup behavior, in J. C. Turner and H. Giles, eds., *Intergroup behavior*, 66–101. Oxford, UK: Basil Blackwell.

Turner, J. C. 1999. Some current issues in research on social identity and self-categorization theories, in N. Ellemers, R. Spears and B. Doosje, eds. *Social identity: Context, commitment, content.* Oxford: Blackwell.

Vanbeselaere, N. 2000. The Treatment of Relevant and Irrelevant Outgroups in Minimal Group Situations With Crossed Categorizations. *Journal of Social Psychology*, 140(4) Aug, 515–527.

Vanbeselaere, N. & Boen, F. 2001. Individual Versus Collective Responses to Membership in a Low-Status Group: The Effects of Stability and Individual Ability. *Journal of Social Psychology*, 141(6) Dec, 765–784.

Vincent, R. C. & Basil, M. D. 1998. College students' news gratifications, media use and current events knowledge. *Journal of Broadcasting & Electronic Media*, 41, Summer, 380–393.

Von Bertalanffy, L. 1952. *Problems of Life: An Evolution of Modern Biological Thought.* New York: Harper.

Weaver, D. H. & Buddenbaum, J. M. 1980. Newspapers and Television: A Review of Research on Uses and Effects, in G. Cleveland and Wilhoit and Harold deBock, eds., *Mass Communication Review Yearbook*, vol. 1. Beverly Hills, CA: Sage, 371–380.

Webster, J. G. 1998. The Audience, *Journal of Broadcasting & Electronic Media*, 42 Spring, 190–208.

Wenner, L. 1986. Model specification and theoretical development in gratifications sought and obtained research: A comparison of discrepancy and transactional approaches. *Communication Monographs*, 53, 160–179.

Westchester County Planning Department, White Plains, NY. Phone interview, 1/5/2003.

Westchester Jewish Conference Research Department, White Plains, NY. Phone interview, 2/10/2003.

Williams, F. 1989. *The New Communications*, 2nd edition. Belmont, CA: Wadsworth.

Worchel, S & Coutant, M, eds. 1998. *Social identity: international perspectives.* London: Sage.

Wright, C. R. 1986. Mass Communication, A Sociological Perspective, 2nd ed. New York: Random House.

Zillmann, D. 1983. Transfer of excitation in emotional behavior, in J. T. Cacioppo and R. E. Petty, eds., *Social Psychophysiology*, 215–240. New York: Guilford Press.

About the Author

Dr. Myna German is Chair of the Department of Communications at Delaware State University. She completed her doctorate at the University of South Africa. She holds a MBA Degree from New York University, M.S. Communications from Boston University, M.Ed., Antioch College, B.A. American Studies, Brandeis University, where she specialized in Religion and Ethnic Studies.

She is a journalist with experience at CBS News and Dow Jones News Service.

The book is based on her doctoral thesis at the University of South Africa in Communication Science.